T0340313

The Feldenkrais Method for Executive Coaches, Managers, and Business Leaders

In this fascinating and practical book, Garet Newell and Simon Paul Ogden show how the Feldenkrais Method can be used by coaches and managers as a resource to improve both the performance of individuals and the health and wellbeing of the people they work with.

The Feldenkrais Method is based on sound mechanical and neurological principles that are easily accessible through simple practical lessons. Through its emphasis on experiential learning, *The Feldenkrais Method for Executive Coaches, Managers, and Business Leaders* offers a means to improve many aspects of everyday working life: from sitting and walking more comfortably, improving interpersonal relations, developing personal impact and presence, to performing a highly developed skill more efficiently. By exploring patterns of everyday movement, the method encourages the discovery of new possibilities and choices providing a remarkable approach for expanding potential.

Although widely recognised within the performing arts and sports as a method for improving skills, performance and recovery from injury, the Feldenkrais Method is not as widely known outside these arenas, yet the principles and practice behind it are equally applicable to the workplace. Using case studies, the book highlights common issues that coaches and managers are frequently asked to deal with. Each case, and the impact it has in the workplace, is explored from the perspective of the Feldenkrais Method. Included at the end of each chapter there is a practical Awareness Through Movement lesson that addresses some of the themes raised.

The Feldenkrais Method for Executive Coaches, Managers, and Business Leaders provides an invaluable resource for professionals interested in both learning and development, and health and wellbeing in the workplace. It will also appeal to counsellors and therapists interested in somatic approaches.

Garet Newell is the educational director of the Feldenkrais International Training Centre in the UK. She studied with Moshe Feldenkrais and became one of the first Europe-based trainers. She has been instrumental in introducing the Feldenkrais Method to a wide variety of people in both the UK and Europe. She played a crucial role in the formation of the International Feldenkrais community, having been a founding member of the International Feldenkrais Federation and of the European Training Accreditation Board.

Simon Paul Ogden is a learning and development practitioner with a background in strategic management consultancy. Specialising in interpersonal communication in business he is also a professional voice and performance coach working with senior executives from some of the UK's leading businesses. He is also a qualified mediator, accredited by Regents College School of Counselling and Psychotherapy.

"This book opens up new avenues for business coaches and practitioners alike – it helps us to take practical steps in making the links between well-being and performance in the workplace. As an approach, its value lies in reminding us that 'self-awareness' tends to be our main barrier to unlocking our potential. With examples taken from real-life and incorporating practical lessons to help us develop our awareness, this book is likely to resonate well with those looking to unleash their own business potential as well as offer useful advice to those typically charged with helping others improve their performance. As an approach to self-development, it is also likely to receive a welcome reception on enlightened MBA programmes."

Dr Anjali Bakhru, BSc(Econ), MBA, PhD; Director of MBA Programmes, Middlesex University, UK

Routledge Focus on Mental Health

Routledge Focus on Mental Health presents short books on current topics, linking in with cutting-edge research and practice.

For a full list of titles in this series, please visit https://www.routledge.com/Routledge-Focus-on-Mental-Health/book-series/RFMH

Titles in the series:

Working with Interpreters in Psychological Therapy
The Right to be Understood
Jude Boyles and Nathalie Talbot

Rational Emotive Behaviour Therapy
A Newcomer's Guide
Walter J. Matweychuk and Windy Dryden

The Feldenkrais Method for Executive Coaches, Managers, and Business Leaders
Moving in All Directions
Garet Newell and Simon Paul Ogden

The Feldenkrais Method for Executive Coaches, Managers, and Business Leaders

Moving in All Directions

Garet Newell and Simon Paul Ogden

With a foreword by Sue Knight

Routledge
Taylor & Francis Group

LONDON AND NEW YORK

First published 2017 by Routledge

2 Park Square, Milton Park, Abingdon, Oxfordshire OX14 4RN

52 Vanderbilt Avenue, New York, NY 10017

Routledge is an imprint of the Taylor & Francis Group, an informa business

First issued in paperback 2019

British Library Cataloguing in Publication Data
A catalogue record for this book is available from the British Library

Library of Congress Cataloging in Publication Data
A catalog record for this book has been requested

ISBN: 978-1-138-23091-0 (hbk)
ISBN: 978-0-367-25164-2 (pbk)

Typeset in Times New Roman
by Swales & Willis Ltd, Exeter, Devon, UK

This book is dedicated to the memory of Moshe Feldenkrais and to all those who are furthering his vision

Contents

Acknowledgements

The process whereby two people come together, collaborate, and write a book, especially one which seeks to bring two specific subjects together in a way that has not been considered extensively before (i.e. the Feldenkrais Method and Learning and Development in the workplace), can be especially complex. In this case the collaboration was much easier than expected. For the sake of clarity:

- Paul took responsibility for writing the text for each chapter, introducing and exploring workplace issues and their impact on health and wellbeing.
- Garet designed and wrote the Awareness Through Movement lessons addressing some of the issues raised and providing a practical example of how the Feldenkrais Method can be used to address the many issues that executive coaches, managers, and business leaders are faced with on a daily basis. In this endeavour we were helped by a number of people who we would like to acknowledge.

Obviously a big thank you to our commissioning editor, Susannah Frearson, from Routledge Focus who first suggested that we might like to submit a proposal to write this book. A second thank you to her for taking it through the editorial panel. Routledge initially published a couple of books by Moshe Feldenkrais including *Body and Mature Behavior: A Study of Anxiety, Sex, Gravitation, and Learning*. It is a privilege to be following in this tradition

Roger Russell, co-director of Feldenkrais Zentrum Heidelberg, provided some early input and advice regarding the neurological aspects of the Feldenkrais Method at the start of this project.

A special thanks to Rebecca Duncombe of Loughborough University for her contribution to Chapter 6 and permission to use her research into early child development.

We are delighted that Sue Knight agreed to write the foreword to this book. Sue is a highly regarded international consultant, author and coach with an outstanding reputation for her role in introducing NLP into the world of business. A big thank you to Julie Willis, senior production editor of Swales & Willis, for her perseverance and resilience in managing the production of this book.

Paul would particularly like to thank Christopher Killick for his comments and support throughout the writing of this book. Imogen Willgress provided some much needed proof reading on the initial draft. And an especial thank you to Janey Blackburn without whose support and input, he would not have been able to contribute to this book.

Foreword

I can count on one hand the number of times in my life when someone doing something has captured the attention of every fibre of my being; when I sensed that what I was experiencing was something way beyond the ordinary and even beyond the great. And that there was something not yet fully untapped in the way it can bring a paradox shift to who we are and the way we think and move. My own business and writing and teaching of NLP (Neuro Linguistic Programming) was based on one such experience and it changed my life not only because of the power of the whole concept but because of the way in which I was able to connect it to the workplace when few, if any, had done the same.

And it was not long after my journey into NLP that I was introduced to Garet Newell an International trainer and practitioner in Feldenkrais, predominantly because I had some physical issues – one being a 'frozen shoulder'. I thought of it initially as just a treatment for the lack of free movement I was experiencing only later to realise very emotionally that it was indeed connected to my self-image and my lack of vision and purpose going forward in my life. What I had never experienced previously was how that realisation came from new movements I was being encouraged to explore. I was gradually seduced into the remarkable world of Moshe Feldenkrais (a man whose genius paralleled others whose thinking and work moved the world forward into a new understanding in line with how we were naturally born to be) and the trainings of my teacher Garet Newell.

And yet the same issue faced this concept of Feldenkrais – of those training in this remarkable approach few had really managed to promote its understanding and application in the world of commerce and business. After all what had physical movement to do with business performance and success?!! The answer is in these pages . . . well certainly the opening to this answer and what a great and timely opening it is. Paul and Garet are a remarkable team in the way that they have united to bring the power and the practicality of Feldenkrais into the minds of those concerned with business performance, fulfilment and success.

Paul and Garet have linked the significance of our self-image and our movement and our attitude to learning to some of the issues that are so commonplace at work – as an example – stress, poor performance and limited potential. And they have done this with clear explanations and links but more importantly with Awareness Through Movement lessons for the reader to try for themselves. As with all natural and generic learning Feldenkrais is experiential and that is the beauty of it. Learning and relearning our natural ways of moving is for us to discover with expert guidance.

I recommend Feldenkrais to nearly everyone I meet who shows signs of interest in discovering how they can create new choices for themselves and subsequently an elegant way of living their life. And now we have this illuminating book to support them in that exploration.

Sue Knight
author of *NLP at Work*
www.sueknight.com

Introduction

Self-knowledge through awareness is the goal of re-education. As we become aware of what we are doing in fact, and not what we say or think, the way to improvements is wide open to us.[1]

Moshe Feldenkrais

It is a simple fact that the majority of us in regular employment have developed habits of working that often deplete our sense of health and wellbeing. Sometimes it appears that the activities we undertake for our own self development, health and wellbeing are outside and separate from the need to make a living; something to be done only if we have the resources and time to do so. The question asked in this book is whether we can learn to work in such a way that increases the sense of curiosity about who we are and allows us to develop in a way that does not have a detrimental impact on our health.

Clearly one of the key roles of the executive coach and business leader is the responsibility to help the people they work with to perform more effectively. Primarily, the goal is to enable them to meet the targets, aims and objectives of the organisation thereby maximising profits and/or the utilisation of resources. Implicit within achieving this goal is the health and wellbeing of the employee. However, the health and wellbeing of an employee is not necessarily the first thing on the mind of the coach or manager when they sit down with their coachee/employee. Quite often this function is seen as the domain of other human resource specialists and/or health practitioners outside the working arena.

Nevertheless the concept of wellbeing in the workplace has developed significantly over the last decade. Increasingly promoted by Government initiatives, the Health and Safety Executive, and professional organisations such as the Chartered Institute of Personnel and Development, the logic is simple, every year businesses are losing, depending on which research you look at, between £30–£50 billion[2] in revenue through absenteeism and presenteeism (i.e. people who turn up for work but who may not be able to perform effectively because of ill health). During the same period of time the actual pressures placed on the workforce have amplified, as the need to maintain and increase profit margins become infinitely harder to achieve during a period of economic uncertainty and financial constraint.

There appears to be very little doubt that these existing and increasing pressures continue to take their toll upon the workforce. At the time of writing, the latest Office for National Statistics Labour Force Survey figures show that the main causes of absenteeism from work are stress/anxiety/depression (approximately 12 million work days each year), and muscular skeletal disorders (approximately 9 million work days each year).

At first it may not seem apparent what coaches and managers can do to improve the health and wellbeing of the people they work with. However, if we consider what most coaching clients ask for assistance with, predominantly the key themes will include; assertiveness, communication skills/emotional intelligence, innovative thinking, impact and presence, influencing skills, resilience, and work life balance. These are all areas in which improvements in performance will generally have a beneficial impact on the levels of stress a person may encounter, together with the muscular skeletal disorders that often occur as the direct result of excess tension.

This book introduces an additional resource that can be used by coaches and managers to achieve the purpose of improving both performance and, the health and wellbeing of the people they work with.

The Feldenkrais Method takes its name from the originator – the scientist Dr Moshe Feldenkrais (1904 – 1984) and is influenced by his expertise in physics, engineering and judo. It is based on sound mechanical and neurological principles that are easily accessible through simple practical lessons. Through its emphasis on experiential learning, the method offers a means to improve many aspects of everyday life – from sitting and walking more comfortably to performing a highly developed skill more efficiently, to easier interpersonal relations. Through exploring patterns of everyday movement, the method encourages the discovery of new possibilities and choices. As a result it provides a remarkable approach for expanding our potential as individuals.

It is a somatic based approach treating the mind and body as one whole. The Method is process rather than goal orientated. It does not prescribe what a person should or shouldn't do, but rather creates an environment in which we can learn and discover what is best for each of us individually, trusting in our own sensations and intelligence (you will discover what this means when you experience the lessons set out in this book). Whilst widely recognised and well regarded within the performing arts and sports as a method for improving skills, performance and recovery from injury, it is not as widely known outside these arenas, and yet the principles and practice behind the Feldenkrais Method are equally applicable to the workplace.

The Method is offered as both group classes (Awareness Through Movement) and individual lessons (Functional Integration). This book primarily focusses on Awareness Through Movement, often referred to as ATMs by practitioners. The movements to be explored are gentle and slow at first, allowing attention to be given to the 'how' of doing an action. This provides the means that enables a person to re-discover, re-learn and re-define the simplicity and ease of everyday movement. Re-organising the muscular skeletal system into a more efficient and healthy whole will have a beneficial impact on the quality of their actions, thoughts, emotions and their overall performance in life.

Layout of the book

Each chapter starts with a short case story highlighting a common issue with which coaches and managers are often presented. The stories are based on actual cases, however, the names and situations have been changed to protect the identity of the individuals and organisations concerned. Each case story is followed by an exploration of the impact the issue has in the work environment, and an examination of the issue from the perspective of the Feldenkrais Method. Each chapter finishes with an Awareness Through Movement (ATM) lesson relevant to the topic under discussion.

The first three chapters consider some of the key theoretical principles behind Moshe Feldenkrais' method, showing their particular relevance to coaching in the work place. The book then follows a structure that closely resembles the learning stages of young children. As Moshe Feldenkrais began to develop his method, he researched the early development of babies and children and found aspects of organic learning which he believed were fundamental to any later experience of learning.

Babies and children explore the world through their senses, are motivated by curiosity and learn new skills through trying out many 'approximations'. This exploration becomes the foundation of further learning. The Feldenkrais Method uses this principle to help individuals develop new skills and to 'perfect' what is already done well.

When observing babies it appears they have a great deal of fun in their explorations. An important principle behind this Method is that learning which is light and joyful is more easily assimilated. There is a lot we can learn from babies, particularly in their attitude towards learning.

- Babies are primarily motivated by their curiosity, their need to connect with their environment and the people in it;
- Babies learn all of their skills by trying out many approximations until they discover one that works most efficiently;
- Babies don't give up when they don't succeed; they take a rest and then try other options;
- Babies learn a new skill SLOWLY until it becomes easy and then they are able to do it more quickly;
- Babies know when to stop and go no further, or to do any more than their current capacity allows them to.

About the lessons

A Feldenkrais practitioner teaches Awareness Through Movement (ATM) through carefully designed lessons. The term exercise is specifically not used as for some people the word evokes the use of repeated effort in order to achieve an end result – for example, improved muscle tone by doing sit ups. Moshe Feldenkrais insisted that movement in the lessons should be light and easy because it is easier to distinguish differences when the effort is light.[3] A lesson implies something is learnt; in this case the aim is to learn ease and efficiency of movement. Moving slowly, using the minimal effort required, refines the ability to sense what is happening and thereby increases awareness. It is the awareness that develops as a result of this re-awakening which improves overall performance and clarity of thinking. This in turn enables us to live a healthier and more fulfilling life. If a movement in any of the lessons within the book feels complicated or requires so much effort that you are holding your breath, it is recommended you stop and imagine doing the movement.

Likewise if you have an injury or disability that prevents you from doing a movement, try doing it in your imagination. This is a technique used by many top sport athletes with great success. The same neural pathways are activated whilst a movement is imagined and has been shown to improve performance and improve muscular tonus[4].

Other practicalities

The starting position for the Awareness Through Movement (ATM) lessons in this book are either lying down, or sitting on a chair. It is important to find somewhere warm and comfortable where you are unlikely to be disturbed. Where the starting position is lying down, a large yoga mat or foam sleeping roll provides the ideal support. In the absence of either, a thick blanket or rug laid out on the floor would also be adequate. Where the starting position is sitting you will need a chair where you can sit forwards towards the edge and have your feet flat on the floor. If the chair is too high you can put something sturdy on the floor to raise your feet, however, whatever you place under your feet should be strong enough to stand on. The easiest way to do the lessons in the book is to read them out aloud and record them for playback later. This will enable you to establish your own pace and will be easier than trying to carry out the movements as you read them from the book. Alternatively you could ask someone else to read them out aloud to you[5].

Notes

1 Taken from the Amherst Training; 2nd July 1980.
2 For example see: PriceWaterhouseCoopers: Building the case for wellness. Report for Department of Work and Pensions; 4 February 2008.
3 Moshe Feldenkrais. *Learning to Learn.* Privately published booklet for Feldenkrais Practitioners 1975.
4 Brian C. Clark, Niladri K. Mahato, Masato Nakazawa, Timothy D. Law, James S. Thomas: The power of the mind: the cortex as a critical determinant of muscle strength/weakness. *Journal of Neurophysiology* Published 15 December 2014 Vol. 112 no. 12, 3219-3226 DOI: 10.1152/jn.00386.2014.
5 Audio copies of the lessons can be obtained from www.feldenkrais-itc.com and www.paulogdencoaching.co.uk

1 Learning to learn (the need for awareness)

Movement is the basis of awareness. Most of what goes on within us remains dulled and hidden from us until it reaches the muscles.[1]

Moshe Feldenkrais

Case story

This first case story differs from the ones which appear in the remainder of this book as it does not relate to an individual who received coaching or had experience of any Feldenkrais lessons. Coaching and mediation was explored as an option to resolve what happened, however, the 'fall out' from the situation was considered so detrimental to the business that another option was adopted. What unfolded in the office of this large international firm is recounted here as occurrences such as this are not uncommon in the workplace. In particular it highlights the need for personal awareness. And the development of awareness is primarily what the Feldenkrais Method is all about – learning Awareness Through Movement thereby increasing sensitivity and attention to one's being.

This case concerns two protagonists – John and Bill. They are senior managers within a customer service department responsible for handling complex enquiries concerning high precision technical engineering machinery. Although they are on the same pay grade, John has been appointed the de-facto manager in overall charge of the operation. Bill may have expected to have been given that role. There is a history of low level antagonism between them which the staff and their director was aware of. When questioned about the incident afterwards the director said he had spoken to both of them previously and had advised them to 'grow up, put their differences to one side, and get on with what they were paid to do'.

Each of them were responsible for a team of around fifty customer service advisors. One morning as Bill was consulting with a team leader, John came over and started to interrupt him, contradicting what he was saying. Bill suddenly snapped and angrily told John to mind his own business and leave him alone. John reacted, immediately getting angry, and they both started exchanging expletives. The main issue concerning their confrontation was that it occurred in the middle of the office, in front of the staff they managed, many of whom where talking to clients around the world. Quite a few of these clients overheard the altercation taking place.

As mentioned above stories such as this are not rare. Everyday there are confrontations between employees, customers, competitors, board directors of the same corrosive nature as the one that took place between John and Bill. The cost is immense and yet the total amount has never been formally calculated. But ask any senior manager and they will talk about the inordinate amount of time they spend on a daily basis 'picking up the pieces' left over from the aftermath of similar interactions and the complaints they generate. There are the interviews with those involved, preparing reports, undertaking disciplinary hearings, dealing with external authorities, mediating between aggrieved parties – and this is with just the minor altercations.

Then there are the working environments where there is underlying conflict between staff – an atmosphere filled with snide remarks and 'back stabbing'. These environments generate an intolerable amount of stress with a detrimental impact on health and wellbeing. They are also the workspaces that have the highest levels of absenteeism and staff turnover. It is surprising just how many people feel that they are powerless to do anything about such environments and consider them to be a 'normal' aspect of everyday working life.

Not many of us are ever likely to meet a person who would say that they want to work in an environment where there is an underlying atmosphere of hostility and aggression. Neither are we likely to meet a person who says 'I want to go into work today and do a really bad job', or, 'I am going to make life really difficult for my colleagues'. Both John and Bill were conscientious and highly respected employees who wanted to do a great job. It just didn't happen on that particular day. Both protagonists lacked the awareness of what they were doing whilst they were doing it.

Over the years many courses have been developed to deal with the type of scenario described above. They have titles such as 'Having Difficult Conversations' and 'Using Conflict Creatively'. All these courses will provide employees and managers with simple tools and ideas that enable them to manage their workspace and relationships with others. One of the key skills developed in these courses is 'Awareness'. It is virtually impossible to have a difficult conversation that 'goes well' or to use conflict creatively without one or other of the parties having developed some degree of self-awareness.

Likewise if you consider the issues that most coaching clients seek assistance with, without awareness it is extremely difficult (if not impossible) to improve performance.

Awareness is a nebulous term – it means many things to many people. People's experience of awareness will vary greatly and this poses its own difficulties when attempting to define what it is. This chapter explores what is meant by awareness from the perspective of the Feldenkrais Method. It also examines how this awareness can help ameliorate situations like the one described above and improve individual and team performance. It also considers how awareness (or a lack of it) impacts on health, safety and wellbeing. Finally it considers the development of awareness which takes place through the observation of patterns of action and the creation of new choices of movement.

The Feldenkrais Method: a definition of awareness and consciousness

Both the words awareness and consciousness are used extensively in both coaching and learning and development interventions. There is often very little distinction given between the two words and they appear so closely interrelated that they are often used interchangeably. In dictionaries the two words are generally used in the definition of the other.

Within the Feldenkrais Method there is a distinct difference between the two words. 'Conscious' can be defined as being awake to one's surroundings. However we all experience different levels of being awake – certainly in relation to our surroundings. We can be 'awake' walking down the road whilst day-dreaming about being on holiday in Australia. Consider the following question from a personal view point – 'at what point between being in deep sleep and being completely wide awake are you truly 'aware' of your surroundings?'

Therefore 'awareness' can be said to be our experience of being 'awake'. How deep is this awareness? How sensitive are you to your surroundings? What is the nature of your attention and intention? Are you able to 'respond' to events as they occur or do you merely 'react' to them as they happen?

The nature of reaction

It is quite clear that both John and Bill were conscious when their altercation took place – they were awake. They had driven into work, had a coffee, and greeted the staff. However, it is the level of their awareness at the time of the confrontation that needs be bought into question. If they had been aware of themselves and the probable outcome that would be the inevitable result of their encounter, would it have ever happened, or would they have found a different way of dealing with their issues?

Both John and Bill were clearly in a state of reaction unable to respond to what was happening at the time. A reaction can be defined as:

Any action that occurs without awareness of a conscious intention.

If, after any interaction, an individual has forgotten what was said or done, or, wish they had said or done something different, then it could be assumed that they have been in a state of reaction. However, is a state of reaction necessarily a bad thing?

Most reactions, especially those of an instinctive nature, are essential for the maintenance and defence of our lives. They comprise the reflexes associated with 'fight flight freeze' response.

If a person accidentally places her/his hand on a burning stove the instinctive reflex will be to pull the hand away. It is only after they have pulled it away that they will become aware of what they have done. The parts of the brain responsible for protection of our being, together with those for handling intense feelings, operate at a much greater speed than the 'higher' systems responsible for thought and abstraction. This mechanism has evolved over millions of years and is necessary for the survival and protection of the human species. Sometimes, however, this mechanism is not quite so useful, especially if, for example, an automatic reaction to intense emotional feelings results in a confrontation similar to the one John and Bill had – an element of self-control is needed. Self-control can only exist with awareness.

If we consider both scenarios described above – placing the hand on the burning stove and John and Bill's confrontation – they raise an interesting question. Why was the person, who was obviously conscious, so unaware of their surroundings that they put their hand on the stove in the first place? Why were John and Bill so unaware of themselves that they reacted in a way that was going to result in behaviour that was eventually considered by their employer to be gross misconduct?

Research has shown that people spend 46.9 per cent of their time thinking about something other than what they are doing. This rises to 50 per cent in the workplace[2]. The implication is that they are not completely aware of what they are doing in the moment. So maybe it is not surprising that 'John and Bill' confrontations are more common than most people would like to think.

Working without awareness

Much of what an individual learns can be brought automatically into action without awareness – especially those activities associated with daily life. These are tasks that have become routine and can be undertaken without thinking about them – for example, making a cup of tea, preparing food, walking to the shop, etc. Skills such as these become 'hard-wired' into the parietal part of our brain. This area of the brain responds automatically to external stimuli at a speed twenty times greater than the frontal cortex which is responsible for logic and thinking. In many respects it can be useful to be able to carry out these routine tasks 'automatically' without any degree of awareness – it is this ability that enables us to multi-task.

Nevertheless there are other skills we may undertake 'automatically' where it might be preferable to perform them with a degree of awareness– for example, driving a car. Many of us will have experienced arriving at a destination with no recollection of driving there. The majority of road traffic accidents occur because of this lack of awareness. Although we may be 'unconsciously competent', the lack of awareness translates into a lack of responsibility, i.e. an inability to respond effectively and engage with our surroundings. Likewise many of the activities required within the workplace can be undertaken without awareness – including the management of self and others.

One of the ways we can consider how skills are learnt and then become 'hard-wired' is through the 'Conscious Competence Learning Model'. It is reintroduced here as it is extensively used in executive training and therefore many coaches and learning and development specialists will be aware of. It provides a set of stages through which the ability to undertake an activity becomes automatic. This in turn points towards a further stage of learning that whilst not included within the model is inherent within the Feldenkrais Method and essential for developing awareness.

The model suggests that when a new skill is learnt an individual will pass through four separate learning stages: stage 1 – 'unconscious incompetence'; stage 2 – 'conscious incompetence'; stage 3 –'conscious competence'; and, stage 4 – 'unconscious competence'. One of the more common analogies used to describe the model is learning to drive a car:

Stage 1: I want to learn to drive and having watched people drive I assume that it is easy.

Stage 2: I get into the car and as I stall it I realise it is a lot more complicated than I thought.

Stage 3: I finally manage to drive the car, keep it on the road without stalling. However, it requires a great deal of concentration and attention.

Stage 4: I can drive the car so well that I can leave the house and arrive at work without having been aware of most of my journey.

Stage 4 is the final stage described in this model. This was considered an ideal point for employers as it meant that their employees were so competent at what they do that they could do it without thinking. In some respects this could well be considered ideal as in stage 3 the level of concentration and time required to undertake a task may result in inefficiencies. Nevertheless, many people have felt uneasy about stage 4 being the final and ideal end state.

The need for a 5th stage

The possible limitation with stage 4 is that it brings a sense of finality over the learning process. It suggests that in relation to the activity there is nothing further to learn, no refinement or ongoing improvement in quality. There is no questioning as to whether what has been learnt still fulfils its original purpose or whether it is still appropriate.

The issue with the model lies within the description of the 4th stage as being 'unconscious'. The implication of this is that a person may be operating automatically without awareness to what is going on around them. Whilst a person may perform 'competently' in this state, arguably they are not operating to their full potential. To go back to the analogy of driving it is the state where most accidents happen.

Up until stage 4 awareness is implicit within the model. We can only move from one stage to another if we have awareness of what we are currently doing and some idea of what we need to do next. The move from a state of unconscious incompetence (stage 1) through conscious incompetence (stage 2) to conscious competence (stage 3) requires the person to have a degree of awareness of themselves, their surroundings, and what they are doing at the time. Then all of a sudden, at stage 4 it appears awareness is no longer required; there is no apparent need for it.

Earlier in this chapter research was introduced that suggested that people spend 50 per cent of their time in the workplace thinking about something other than what they are doing. If this is the case we are operating without complete awareness. It is also possible that many of us have spent the greater part of our life operating in this state. If we are working without awareness we are unlikely to have any foresight of the probable or possible outcome of our actions.

Therefore many of the actions we perform on a daily basis may no longer be as efficient or as useful as when we first learnt them. Because of the way they are hard-wired into the parietal part of the brain, they become habits. Habits need to be adaptable to contexts that are different from the situations in which they were originally learnt. When they are not they may significantly affect our emotional and physical well-being.

Movement without awareness

The way in which we move, our postures, the way in which we hold our-selves, have been learnt at one time or another and will have become habitual. Generally these habits of movement suit a purpose. They may still suit the purpose they were originally intended for but sometimes they may not. The following story highlights the phenomena.

Case story

Shirley is in her early forties and to all appearances seems very presentable, personable and outgoing. However, she suffers from a constant pain in her middle back. She has lived with the pain for as long as she can remember. It is a chronic pain that has become debilitating and tiring over time. Over the years Shirley has had countless X-rays, scans, and numerous consultations with special-ists. Nobody ever found the cause for the pain or anything wrong with her. The only relief she got from the pain was a fortnightly session with her Chiropractor.

Her ability to work as a consulting forensic accountant was suffering as a result of the continuous pain. She found it hard to concentrate at the level she needed to. Over the last few years she had been passed over for promotion. Her personal relationships suffered. Most of her relationships lasted less than three years. She described herself as volatile and emotional, getting upset over the smallest of issues. She put all this down to the constant pain she was feeling. A friend suggested she try the Feldenkrais Method.

After several sessions of Functional Integration (one-to-one les-sons with a practitioner), it had transpired that as a child she had damaged her right ankle quite severely. Whilst it would be barely perceptible to the general observer, this had resulted in her devel-oping a way of walking that prevented her from feeling the pain of her injury and had helped her to recover. This way of moving became habitual and influenced how she walked. At the time she adopted the movement it served a useful purpose, however, forty years later it became one of the primary sources of her back pain.

The way she was walking restricted movement in her pelvis, plac-ing increased pressure on her spine and shoulder girdle, resulting in the pain in her back. By re-learning to walk in a way that was more comfortable and efficient, she gained more fluidity of movement in her pelvis and the back pain vanished. This enabled a re-organisation of her muscular-skeletal functioning which not only helped her breathing but made her able to be quieter, comfortable and relaxed. In this revised way of moving she discovered a new emotional balance that enabled her to start living her life in the way she wanted. People in her social circle found it easier to be with her, and her relationships improved providing her with a greater sense of confidence.

The 5th stage: awareness of action

Most of our habits, both in movement and behaviour, have been learnt and developed in response to circumstances over many years. Without awareness, the impact that these habits have on the quality of our life, health and wellbeing, are subject to chance. The majority of the time there may be no serious repercussions; however, occasionally a lack of awareness can change the whole course of person's life.

In the case of John and Bill's interaction in the office we can safely surmise that if either one of them had been working with a degree of awareness the outcome of their confrontation would have been different. As it was, both of them were dismissed from their employment.

'Learning to learn', which was referred to in the introduction, was a booklet written by Moshe Feldenkrais in 1975 as a 'manual to help practitioners to get the best results from the Awareness Through Movement Lessons'. In it he suggests a way of action that does not rely on concentration but encourages us to 'attend well to the entire situation, yourself, and your surroundings by scanning the whole sufficiently to become aware of any change or difference, concentrating just enough to perceive it'.

Awareness of action is a somatic state that allows attention to focus on what is being done as it occurs without undue 'emotional' interference. It enables the individual to continuously evaluate what they are doing and how they are doing it, enabling them to refine their actions in the present moment using feedback from their surroundings. It is a state of awareness achieved by the best performers in sport, theatre and music. It is the state that enables the outstanding actor to play the same role night after night whilst engaging the audience in the illusion that what is happening on stage is happening for the first time. It is also the state of awareness that is experienced by some of the best performers in business. Going back to the analogy of driving it is the state of the advanced driver.

An advanced driver transcends the unconscious competence of Stage 4. The advanced driver is not thinking about anything other than driving the car, fully alert to what is going on ahead, behind and to the side, reading the road. Driving in this state is a skill that has to be learnt – it involves re-learning to drive with awareness. People who have passed their advanced driving test will tell you how much harder it was than they were expecting. As they re-learnt to drive they found they had developed all sorts of habits that had resulted in them becoming less than competent drivers.

Likewise to refine and become increasingly competent in any action we undertake requires awareness and as we use our awareness we will often find ourselves re-learning some of the most basic actions we take for granted. However, awareness of action enables a person undertake their daily activities in a more effective and efficient way, and, with practice, this state is achievable by everyone.

The Feldenkrais Method offers an approach for any of us engaged in the coaching of others – it develops awareness in action through Awareness Through Movement.[3]

Awareness Through Movement lesson: becoming aware of your preferences

All the instructions for movement will generally be given as if you were standing (even when you are lying on the floor), so, for example, moving the shoulder forwards, when you are lying on your back, in a spatial reference, is moving it towards the ceiling. The instructions will be given, however, as if you are in a standing position.

The instructions are meant to be followed in a particular manner: do each one slowly; stop just before you feel yourself making any unnecessary effort in order to go further; repeat each movement several times and rest in between each instruction and the next. If any of the movements are at all painful, don't carry them out, but 'imagine' doing them. If you put too much effort into the movement, you will reduce the degree of sensation that you can feel.

Find a quiet space where you will not be disturbed for at least thirty minutes. Slowly bring yourself to lie down on your back with your legs long and your arms lying at your side.

Diversity is an issue that all coaches work with and it equally applies in movement. For example while a person might assume that everyone would lie in a similar way, the opposite tends to be the case: for example, some people will have their palms of their hands upwards, sideways, downwards, or somewhere in between. Peoples' arms will be at varying distances from their sides, the toes of their feet pointing in different directions.

Slowly become aware of yourself lying on the floor. Observe the contact you make with the floor, starting with the heels of your feet and moving up to the back of your head. Notice also which areas don't make any contact with the floor. Are you contacting the floor with the same amount of weight on your right side as on your left side? Take a moment to notice where you can feel movement in response to your in breath and to your outbreath.

'Know thyself' and 'an unexamined life is not worth living' are quotations ascribed to the ancient Greek philosopher Socrates. Both phrases of advice are generally taken to relate to understanding ourselves psychologically (making sense of our emotional reactions) and sociologically (how we relate to those around us). Only rarely do we consider self-knowledge from a kinaesthetic point of view.

- slowly start to bend the toes of one foot in the direction of the top of the foot. How easy do you find it to bend them? Do they all bend the same amount? Which foot did you choose? Do this movement a number of times.
- now do the same bending of the toes with your other foot. Do the toes move differently on this foot?

Stop and rest.

- begin to bend your ankle so that the top of your foot moves towards your lower leg; we will call this 'upwards'. Are your toes bending at the same time? Can you bend just the ankle without bending the toes? Remember to do the amount of bending that feels comfortable and to stop at the point where to go further you would need to use more effort.

Many of our daily actions are what we can call 'undifferentiated'. If you find that your toes bend at the same time as you are directing your ankle to bend, both are moving at the same time, as the two movements are connected together in your image of this movement in the part of your brain, called the motor cortex. The two movements are not what is described as 'differentiated' i.e. you can do one separately

(continued)

(continued)

from the other. You will be surprised how many movements are bound together in this manner. They can also be described as 'parasitic' actions, not belonging to the intention.

- as you continue to bend your ankle upwards, can you feel your heel move away and the back of your lower leg getting longer? How far can you feel this movement upwards along your leg? Can you feel it in your upper leg? Which foot did you spontaneously decide to move?
- now do the same movement of bending the ankle upwards with the other foot. Repeat this a few times. Does your ankle seem to bend more, or less, on this side?
- bend your ankle once with the foot you used first, then once with the foot you used second and compare if anything feels different.

Stop and rest.

Understanding and experiencing movement are important elements in 'knowing thyself'. As discussed earlier, movement cannot be easily separated from our emotional or intellectual states. It is very hard to imagine a brain without a body. When we act, we act as a whole and in some respects it is unhelpful (and unhealthy) to conceptually separate our body from our mind and emotions and treat it as a distinct entity. However, it is a part of ourselves that many of us know very little about until we become ill or incapacitated in some way or another — or decide that it might be an interesting pursuit!

- choose one leg and begin to slowly roll it inwards and then let it return. Allow your heel to stay in the same place while gently rolling your leg and keep your leg straight. Repeat this movement several times. Can you feel the movement 'travelling' all the way up to your hip joint?
- now do the same movement with your other leg. Does it roll differently, or more easily? If one leg is rolled further outwards to begin with, rolling each leg will feel different.
- now roll the leg you moved first, followed by the leg you moved second and you can feel more clearly now if there are any differences.

Stop and rest.

- roll one leg outwards to the point where it doesn't roll any further unless your knee bends slightly outwards, allow your knee to bend, then allow your leg to return until it is straight again. Repeat this several times, slowly. Feel the movement now in your upper leg as well as in your hip joint. Do you notice that the weight in your pelvis is also gradually increasing on that side?
- roll the other leg outwards, again reaching the place where you can bend your knee outwards and you feel a movement of rotation in your hip joint. Slowly straighten your leg and return it to the starting position. Repeat this movement several times, noticing also a shift of weight in your pelvis. Is this movement easier on this side, or on the first one?

Stop and rest.

We all have an image of ourselves that affects our relationships with others and it will often have very little correlation to reality. As an experiment, consider your height in relation to those around you. Are you taller or shorter? Can you find someone who is the same height as your image of yourself? You may be surprised that when you stand next to this person, they are actually shorter or taller than you!

- slowly and very gently lift one side of your pelvis, moving it forward, then let it return. You will need to find certain specific muscles which make this movement possible without making any 'extraneous' efforts. Refrain from making efforts with your legs. Feel that the weight rolls to the other side of your pelvis in order to make this movement, which is a rotational movement of your pelvis around your spine – or your vertical axis.
- begin to lift the other side of your pelvis, bringing it forwards and feeling the weight roll to the opposite side. Repeat this movement several times, finding the specific muscles which make this possible. You may find that one of these directions of rotation is easier than the other. The muscles which make this movement possible may be more accustomed to contracting on one side than on the other.

(continued)

(continued)

Stop and rest.

In the previous movement of bringing one side, then the other, of the pelvis forwards, you may have noticed a significant difference in the ease of the movement in one direction. You may have felt that you 'couldn't locate' or 'bring into action' the muscles on one side in comparison to the other. These differences mostly go unnoticed until you find the opportunity to discover them. A preference in rotation is an important factor in the origin of discomfort or even pain which occurs on one side, but not, seemingly, on the other side. You may bring together now your experience of rolling one leg outwards until you could bend that knee and the movement of bringing the pelvis forwards and discover if there is a relationship between the two. Often the leg which rolls more easily outwards will be the same side as the direction in which it is easier to move one side of your pelvis backwards. Both of these movements may reveal preferences that show up in the direction in which you turn more easily – an important factor in performance in dance or sports, for example.

–   roll your pelvis so that you exaggerate the curve in your lower back; we can call this rolling it 'forwards'. The upper part of the front of your pelvis is the part actually moving forwards. You will feel the lower back muscles contracting and your abdomen going forwards, then let go and return to the starting position. As you repeat this movement slowly and gently, you may feel a slight increase of pressure in your upper back, at the level of the shoulder blades, as well as a change in the curve in the back of your neck and a slight movement of your head. Notice if this movement is any easier if you breathe in at the same time that you are making a curve in your lower back.
–   now, roll your pelvis in the opposite direction, which we will call 'backwards', so that you lengthen and flatten your lower back towards the floor. You will feel a response in your legs, as well as in your neck along with a slight movement of your head. Notice if this movement feels easier to do while breathing out.

Stop and rest.

Notice if there is any difference in the contact you are making with the floor now. Are any parts of you lying with more weight, or area of contact?

Some of the key muscles used for movement are in groupings, called flexors and extensors. They are skeletal muscles meaning that they attach to bones and interact with the joints to generate movement. They can be controlled voluntarily. When doing the movement of exaggerating the arch in the lower back, it is primarily the extensor muscles on both sides of the lower spine that are engaged to make this possible. When doing the movement of flattening the lower back, the flexor muscles in the front of the torso, mainly in the abdomen are engaged to make this movement possible.

– bring your attention to your arms and notice what part of you lower arm lies in contact with the floor. Are the palms of your hands turned forwards (towards the ceiling), or backwards (contacting the floor) or are they lying on the outside part of your hand towards the smallest finger, with the thumbs upwards and the palms of your hands towards the side of your pelvis or upper legs? As mentioned previously, everyone will have their own pattern of placing their arms at their sides while lying on the back, close to one of the three possibilities described.
– roll one forearm inwards a few times. This movement is one of the two bones of the lower arm rotating around one another; then roll the same arm outwards. Depending on your starting organisation, you will have more movement in one direction of rolling than in the other. Although this movement is primarily in the lower arm, can you feel any sensations in your upper arms and in your shoulder joints?
– do the same movements with your other arm. Do you have more, or less, range of movement in this arm?

Stop and rest.

This movement will make it obvious that most people use one arm and hand differently to the other. In your early development you chose, or were encouraged to choose to hold utensils, then drawing and writing 'tools' in either your right or your left hand. This developed an ability and skill on one side and not on the other. This is called 'dominance' and is very crucial in the development of motor skills. If you spend a lot of time at a computer and only use your dominant hand to guide the 'mouse', then you can develop a repetitive

(continued)

(continued)

strain injury. This may manifest as pain in the wrist, lower arm, even shoulder and neck on one side.

- lift one shoulder, bringing it forwards. Feel how this creates a slight rotation in the upper torso and that the weight shifts a little to the other side. Repeat this several times, noticing if your head rolls slightly, or if it stays in the middle.
- now lift the other shoulder, bringing it forwards. Which one moves forwards more easily? Does your head respond differently? Is it the same side as your 'dominant' hand?

Stop and rest.

- roll your head slowly and gently in one direction. Stop at the point where you would have to use further effort and notice where the tip of your nose is pointing. Repeat this several times, staying within the range of easy movement.
- roll your head now in the other direction and notice the point at which you stop. Is it further or less distance than with the first direction? Where does the tip of your nose point on this side?

Stop and rest.

- tilt your head, so that your ear comes closer to your shoulder on the side you chose to do it first. You will also feel the back of your head slide in an arc-like movement along the floor. Return and then repeat this movement slowly a number of times as it can be challenging for the neck vertebrae to move in this manner. Be sure that your nose stays pointing to the ceiling, so that you are not also rotating your neck vertebrae at the same time.
- tilt your other ear towards the other shoulder, feeling the sliding movement of the back of your head on the floor and return. Do this several times, slowly and stopping at the point where the movement is still easy.

Stop and rest.

You may notice that with this movement, you can tilt your head more easily in one direction. This could be the result of habit – if you hold a telephone to one ear or carry or wear a bag on one side. The neck and upper spine will then curve more easily in this direction. If just a small tilt of the weight of your head in one direction becomes habitual, there may be ways in which this reflects in your jaw, and your overall balance.

– slowly move your chin away from your chest while sliding the back of your head on the floor and looking upwards. Keep your jaw closed and feel the arch this makes in your neck and your cervical spine, then bring your head back to the starting place. Repeat this movement a number of times.
– move your chin towards your chest, feeling the back of your head slide on the floor and the back of your neck lengthen and flatten in the direction of the floor, and your eyes look downwards, then return. Do this movement a number of times. Does this direction of movement feel more familiar to you than the previous one?

Slowly bring yourself up to sitting and then to standing. Does anything feel different to you? Are you more aware of the various places you moved and paid attention to? Is there anything different in your image of yourself?

This lesson is designed for you to 'get to know yourself'. Most of the movements are ones that you do every day, though they have been simplified in order to feel them more easily. You may have been surprised at the differences in the movements to the right and to the left, towards the floor and away from the floor, some of which you may have become aware of for the first time. Once you become aware of your own preferences, you can 'play' with them so that they don't become 'fixed' in habitual patterns.

Notes

1 Moshe Feldenkrais (1990). *Awareness through movement: easy to do exercises to improve your posture, vision, imagination, and personal awareness.* New York: HarperCollins.
2 Killingsworth, M A and Gilbert, D T (2010). *A wandering mind is an unhappy mind.* Cambridge, MA: Harvard University.
3 Clark D, Schumann F and Mostofsky S H (2015). Mindful movement and skilled attention. *Frontiers in Human Neuroscience.* 9:297

2 The development of self image

The way a man holds his shoulders, head, and stomach; his voice and expression; his stability and manner of presenting himself – all are based on his self-image.[1]

Moshe Feldenkrais

Case story

Karl is a young man who has recently been promoted to Marketing Manager of a major international manufacturing firm. He is responsible for promoting a range of products that will be used within the oil industry.

As part of this role he has been asked to present a new product to the annual European sales conference. The presentation will be in front of over a thousand sales executives and managers. He is so scared about having to do this presentation that, as a result of the stress he is feeling, he has agreed with his wife that he will hand in his notice and look for a new job. They have two young children and whilst she has no income he cannot see any other alternative – he has been told by his managers that he has to do the presentation regardless of his feelings. They have, however, arranged for him to receive some coaching.

Karl originally joined this company at the age of 16, straight from leaving school. He was employed on the factory floor making the goods he would later go on to market. After several years as a section leader he transferred into the office, first working in the sales department before moving into marketing. Whilst he has some experience of presenting to small groups of people this is the first time he has ever been asked to make such a large presentation. He has come in for the coaching session even though he has been signed off work by his doctor due to stress. What is particularly noticeable is the impact this is having on his personal health and wellbeing – in addition to the anxiety he is feeling, he is suffering from chronic lower back pain and is having difficulty walking. He is also having difficulty speaking as a result of constriction in his throat.

Ability and health

The introduction highlighted some of the key themes that coaches and managers are often asked to help individuals address. These include: assertiveness, communication skills, emotional intelligence, innovative thinking, impact and presence, influencing skills, resilience, and work life balance.

More often than not it is possible to discern a direct link between a lack of ability in any of these skills and ill health, particularly ill health relating to stress and muscular skeletal disorders. This is clearly apparent in Karl's story and there are plenty of other people in the workplace who suffer from ill health brought on through the anxiety of their self-perceived or actual lack of ability.

If, as a result of a coaching intervention, a person finds it easier to achieve something that they were previously having difficulty with, then the coach will have helped them become a healthier person.

There are many different types of coaching interventions using a wide variety of psychological models, skills and techniques that enable individuals to change the way they think or emotionally react to a situation. Every coach will have their own favourite ways of working, all of which are used because they have proved to be effective.

As explained in the introduction, the Feldenkrais Method provides an additional approach for considering, observing and analysing individual performance and the impact it has on personal wellbeing. From this analysis it is possible for a Feldenkrais Practitioner to introduce a learning intervention through an Awareness Through Movement lesson or a one to one Functional Integration session, that will open up a whole new range of possibilities that can influence performance and improve overall health and wellbeing.

How this is achieved is best explained through one of the key principles underlying the Feldenkrais Method. This principle proposes that every action undertaken in daily life consist of the following elements, namely: thinking, feeling (emotion), sensation and movement. Each of these elements are always present to some degree or another in every thing we do. Each have a direct relationship with the other. For example if a person undertakes an action that makes them feel anxious, the feeling (emotion) associated with the anxiety will have a corresponding thought, a sensation, and a postural expression (movement). Moshe Feldenkrais proposed that if we want to change any of these elements, for example, the emotion, the easiest and most accessible way to do this is through creating a change in the habitual pattern of movement. This particular principle will be explored in more detail in the next chapter and throughout the remainder of the book. In the meantime Karl's reaction to being asked to do something he personally found overwhelming allows us to explore Moshe Feldenkrais' thoughts about 'self-image'.

Karl and the concept of self image

At the time of his initial coaching session, from the perspective of the Feldenkrais Method, Karl's personal 'self image' did not contain the potential to stand up in front of a more than a thousand sales executives and make a presentation. He did not have that image of himself because he had never had to speak in public to a large audience before. Neither had he received any training that would enable him to do so. Without the experience from the past to draw upon to achieve the objective required in the present moment, it is unlikely that any action will be accomplished with ease.

For Moshe Feldenkrais an understanding of an individual's self image and how it had evolved was a key towards assisting the person in developing their personal potential. His model of self image is practical and has stood the test of time from both a psychological and sociological point of view. Whilst it does have many similarities to other models that address the need for self-awareness it also contains some unique characteristics.

In the Feldenkrais Method 'self image' is the way we perceive ourselves in relationship to the society and culture in which we live and operate. It will manifest itself in our actions and in how we think, feel, sense and move. It will be inherent in the way we walk and talk. Our self image is reflected within our posture and how we relate to all those around us. Each of us has a self image that is truly unique. The self image of a person who speaks five different languages will be different to a person who speaks only one. The self image of a top classical pianist will be different to that of the jazz pianist. And, to reinforce the point, Karl's self image was completely different from that of his immediate line manager who had previously made successful presentations to large numbers of clients and colleagues.

An individual's self image begins to develop from birth. It may even start to develop before this whilst in the womb and there is certainly a great deal of research which shows that early learning starts in utero.[2] Self image is primarily the product of our early learning, although it will continue to develop as we grow older. We learn at an incredibly fast rate when we are children; we need to in order to survive. We learn to walk, talk and socialise; the skills that enable us to integrate into the society in which we have been born. The majority of this early learning will determine the way we interrelate with others for the rest of our lives. It will also colour the assumptions we make in our interactions with others.

In Chapter 5 the case story concerns Chrissie, the operations director of a medium sized company that is experiencing financial difficulties. The chapter primarily considers issues concerning healthy eye sight and the effect that working with digital screen technology can have on our mental health and productivity. However one aspect of the story worth considering at this point was how she assumed that her rescue plan for the business had been badly received by the chairman and chief executive. This assumption has been based on the fact that she had seen them whispering to each other and, in her mind, obviously ignoring her. The rest of the board had sat through her presentation in complete silence. She interpreted this negatively and felt that her presentation had been a disaster.

She was perceiving what had happened through the lens of her self image. She was making assumptions based on her own interpretation of the world as it stood at that moment. This was adversely affected by the hours she had spent working in the office without taking appropriate breaks. In a subsequent meeting with the chief executive she mentioned that she had noticed his conversation with the chairman whilst she was presenting her key points. She asked him if there was anything he would like her to clarify. He laughed and explained that he had turned to the chairman to comment on how good her report was and that they would need to carry out her recommendations in full. His final comment to her was that the presentation had been outstanding – there had not been one murmur from the team all the way through.

Most of us will make assumptions based on the 'reality' of our own self image – how we perceive the environment and how we assume others perceive us. In order to develop personally we need to question our assumptions – we need to be curious about our relationship with our environment. We need to understand our self image and how it plays out in daily life.

The need for curiosity

Once we meet the expectations that our immediate environment places on us, many of us will stop developing our potential. This is because we have achieved all that is necessary for our immediate survival. The expectations placed on us will be unique depending on location, upbringing, education, peer pressure, etc. Moshe Feldenkrais suggested that the expectations of society and the individual's need to conform to them could well place limitations on the development of our potential. He believed that the people held up as geniuses should not be considered as exceptional, as we all have the potential to be geniuses if we continually question the perceived wisdom of the day – or even question the limits of our own wisdom.

Moshe Feldenkrais observed that many people seem to lose their sense of curiosity. It is possible that as most of what we learn and believe develops at an early age, at a later age we consider that what we have become is all that we can reasonably expect to be. In other words we believe that we have already achieved all that we are capable of. However it is never too late to learn and develop new skills and apply them well – for example, to learn to play the piano, speak another language, or even to make a presentation to more than a thousand sales executives at a European sales conference for the first time.

Whilst it is apparent that some people are born with a natural predilection, and often physique, towards a certain way of life and living[3], how these predilections develop are more often to do with nurture and the society in which we find ourselves. What Moshe Feldenkrais asks is this; regardless of our nature and how we have been nurtured, how much more can we become? Is it possible to expand our self image?

We are all brought up with a fairly concrete perception of what society requires from us in order to fit in. It becomes part of our self image and as a result many of us may only value ourselves to the extent we believe our society values us. We have to make our way in the world to ensure our personal survival and if we feel that the society in which we belong (or have chosen to belong) does not value us, it has a severe impact on our health and well being. This is especially true in our relationship with the workplace.

Naturally our personal values and beliefs and how we perceive ourselves plays a major part in the development of our potential. Not all of us value music to the extent we would want to learn to play the piano. However, what happens if our self image has developed in a way that prevents us from being able to achieve those things we value and believe in?

One of the interesting outcomes that may arise from any form of coaching is where the individual discovers that their employment does not correlate with their values and beliefs. Any form of personal development that works with self-awareness may result in this phenomena and when it does, whilst the life changing results should be positive, it could well feel disconcerting for all those involved.

Hopefully most of us are able to make a living in a way that has personal value to our lives. However, whatever we do there will be times when we will come across personal limitations in our ability. In Karl's case that was the requirement placed on him by his immediate line manager to make a presentation to more than a thousand sales executives.

Any limitation we become aware of has the potential to effect our health and ability to fulfil the requirements of our work. In Karl's case his personal self image was such that he could not believe he had the potential to make his presentation. Actually he did have the ability. All he needed to do was to become more aware of himself and recognise his potential.

Karl received specific presentation coaching and was also advised to undertake some Feldenkrais lessons. Karl made his presentation to the European sales conference and it was very well received. He is now one of the company's key presenters responsible for the launch of all new products in Europe. Karl was given two lessons – the first was similar to that given in the first chapter and it was suggested he should do it every day and treat it as a 'meditation'. The second lesson he was given is similar to the one set out below.

Awareness Through Movement lesson: refining your self image

There are many short lessons in 'Awareness Through Movement' that aid in refining the self image. Many people only use a limited range of movements that the human body is capable of. Staying safe, not wanting to stand out, feeling awkward, along with an attachment to familiarity are some of the ways in which every day movement becomes habitual. There are simple ways in which the capacity for wider ranges of movement can be enhanced and performance improved. This lesson is one such way.

During this lesson it is important to repeat each movement several times, not for the sake of 'exercise', but for the opportunity to sense all the different parts of yourself that get involved and to feel when you are reaching the limit of movement which is comfortable.

Lie on your back with your legs straight and slightly spread apart and both arms lying at your sides. If you cannot lie comfortable with your legs straight, or if that position is painful, you can do this lesson with your legs bent with knees balanced over your ankles and adapt the instructions accordingly.

Bring your left arm to lie above your head in a comfortable place, with the back of your hand on the floor, bending it slightly at the elbow. Don't worry if your entire arm doesn't touch the floor – just so that some part of the back of your hand does.

(continued)

(continued)

- begin to slide your left arm, the parts which are in contact with the floor over to the right. As you do, you will find that you need to bend your right side, shortening the distance between your right shoulder and the right side of your pelvis, bringing the ribs closer together. Then slide your arm back to that comfortable place above your head. Repeat this several times.
- stay with your left arm above your head and slightly over to the right, this time, bend it more so that you can take your left wrist with your right hand – the back of your right hand is on the floor and back of the left hand is resting in the palm of your right hand, the thumb and first finger of your right hand holds on either side of the two bones of the lower left arm — just next to where most people wear their watches. With both arms bent at the elbow, take the left arm further to the right by 'pulling' gently with your right hand and then bring it back to where you started.
- repeat this several times. You will feel your entire upper spine – your head, neck and chest bending to the right; let your eyes and the tip of your nose stay facing towards the ceiling. The movement is in one plane; a 'pure' side bending, with both shoulders remaining on the floor.

Stop and rest, let your arms lie at your side. Notice when you return to lying on your back if the space between your shoulder and pelvis feel equal on the right and on the left sides.

Whenever we bend to one side, then return to the middle, it can create a sensation of that side 'feeling shorter', even though, objectively, it may not be shorter.

Spread your legs slightly and bring your left arm above your head again.

- take the left wrist with the right hand, as you did in the previous step, slide everything over to the right again and this time stay where the amount of bending is comfortable.
- now, slide your straight left leg along the floor in the direction of your right leg, only as far as it is easy, as this will lengthen your left side. Slide your left leg back and then towards the right leg again. Repeat this several times.

Stop and rest. Let go of everything and return to the starting position. Don't be surprised if you feel a bit 'banana-shaped'.

Spread your legs, bring your left arm overhead and begin to slide your left arm to the right, bend your torso so that you can stay in this position; let your right arm be alongside you, as if reaching down towards your right foot.

- slide your left leg again towards your right leg so that your left side is lengthened. Stay in this position; you will want to feel that you are bent as far as is comfortable to the right and lengthened as far as is comfortable on your left side.
- begin to do a movement, like a see-saw, alternately expanding your chest, then expanding your abdomen. As you do this, you want to have the image of the roundness of your chest and abdomen, so when you expand, they get larger in the front, sides and back. There will be a big difference in this movement on the right side, which is bent and shorter and the left side which is expanded and longer. You don't need to think about coordinating your breathing with this movement, but be sure that you are not holding your breath – and your breathing will take place naturally. In between your chest and the top of your pelvis sits the diaphragm, the breathing muscle.

Stop and rest and return to lying in the middle with both arms at your sides.

The movement of alternately expanding your chest, then your abdomen, allows any muscles which are extended, as on the side which is lengthening, or contracted, as on the side which is shortening to be more comfortable in these positions. These movements also have the effect of 'freeing' the diaphragm muscle, which then allows for fuller breathing.

Spread your legs, bring your left arm overhead again.

- take your left wrist with your right hand and slide both arms over to the right, so that you are again bent to your right.
- slide your left leg again towards your right leg so that your left side is lengthened; leave the left leg where it can stay comfortably while lengthening the left side. Notice if it is a bit easier to be in this position. Now, slide the right leg further to the right and back to where it was. Repeat this movement a number of times to notice how it affects the shortening of the right side and the lengthening of the left side.

(continued)

(continued)

Stop and rest. Return to lying with your arms at your sides.

The starting position may feel a bit different to how it did at the beginning. Even though you have returned to your 'middle', you may still sense that one side feels longer and one side feels shorter. This is a great illustration of a phenomenon of perception. The feeling of your 'middle' may be difficult to find again, due to the repeated one-directional side bending. Many people have habits of bending more to one side than the other and this becomes habitual in a way that it is no longer perceived. However this is a 'fresh' experience of creating a difference between your two sides.

Bend your legs so that your feet are standing, roll to one side and slowly find a way to come to sitting, then to standing. In standing, shift your weight from your right leg to your left leg and feel any differences.

In standing, with your arms at your side, slide your right palm down along the outside of your right leg and feel how far it goes and how the right side bends. Come back and slide your left palm down the outside of your left leg and feel how far it goes easily and how your left side bends. Bend your head so that your right ear moves towards your right shoulder. Now bend so that your left ear moves towards your left shoulder. You will find a noticeable difference between this side bending movement on each side. Walk around and notice if you step differently on one foot than on the other.

With this lesson, you have created a difference between the right and left sides, with which you may feel off balance, awkward and certainly not your familiar self. If you feel comfortable, or if it feels interesting to remain like this, you may stop now and enjoy the sensations of each side feeling different. If not, please continue the lesson which will now perform the same movements in the other direction.

Lie on your back with your legs slightly spread, bring your right arm to lie above your head with the back of your right hand on the floor:

– slowly slide your right arm over to the left, sensing how your left side bends, shortening the distance between your left shoulder and the left side of your pelvis, and the right side lengthens. Do this several times.
– stay with your right arm above your head, bend it at the elbow so that you can take your right wrist with your left hand, holding just above (in the direction of your elbow) the two bones of your lower right arm so that you can slide both arms to the left, then

bring them back. Repeat this several times, feeling your entire left side bending to the left, being sure to keep your eyes looking at and your nose pointing to the ceiling.

Stop and rest. Let your arms lie at your sides. Notice if the distance between your left shoulder and left side of your pelvis feels different than that between your right shoulder and right side of your pelvis.

Spread your legs slightly again and bring your right arm above your head where it can lie comfortably.

– take the right wrist with your left hand and slide everything over to the left again and stay where it is comfortable, slide your right leg along the floor in the direction of your left leg and bring it back. Feel the lengthening along your right side. Repeat this several times.

Stop and rest with your arms at your side. You may already feel, although you have returned to the 'middle', that you remain slightly bent over to the left side.

Spread your legs, bring your right arm overhead and slide it to the left so that you can stay there; leave your left arm at your side, as if reaching downwards towards your left foot.

– slide your right leg towards your left leg, so that you can feel your right side getting longer. Repeat this several times, then stay in this bent position and begin to alternately expand your chest, then your abdomen, separating this movement from that of breathing in and out.

Stop and rest, return to lying in the middle with your arms at your sides.

Spread your legs, bring your right arm overhead again.

– take your right wrist with your left hand and slide both arms over to the left and stay in this bent position, then slide your right leg again towards your left one, so that your entire right side lengthens. Repeat this movement several times, then stay with the right leg closer to the left one. Now slide your left leg away from your right one, further to the left, then back. Repeat this movement several times, noticing how the left side shortens even further.

(continued)

(continued)

Stop and rest. Return to lying with your arms at your sides. Bend your legs so that your feet are standing, roll to one side and slowly find a way to come to sitting, then to standing. In standing, shift your weight from your left leg to your right leg. Slide your left palm down the outside of your left leg and feel how much more easily your right side bends now. Slide your right palm down the outside of your right leg. Do you feel more alike on each side? Walk around and notice if your walk is more balanced now.

Notes

1 Moshe Feldenkrais, (1990). *Awareness through movement: easy to do health exercises to improve your posture, vision, imagination, and personal awareness,* p.23. New York: HarperCollins
2 For example see: Alexandra R Webb, Howard T Heller, Carol B Benson, and Amir Lahav (2015). *Mother's voice and heartbeat sounds elicit auditory plasticity in the human brain before full gestation.* Edited by Mortimer Mishkin. Bethesda, MD: National Institute for Mental Health
3 Iacono, William G and McGue, Matt (2012). Minnesota twin family study. *Twin Research.* 5 (05): 482–487.

3   The question of performance

No matter how closely we look, it is difficult to find an action that can take place without the support of some physical function.[1]

Moshe Feldenkrais

Case story

'What a stunning performance. He was brilliant. He knew exactly what he was doing and what needed to be done. On a personal level he was there for every one of us. He was calm and collected and listened to all our points of view. He spoke with conviction and was positive. If I could become half the leader he is I would be happy. I would follow his lead anywhere'.

Phillip is talking about Simon, his direct line manager. They work for a large international pharmaceutical company. This company had recently acquired a new business and the merger of the two very different cultures had not gone particularly well. The reason for the acquisition had been to expand research and development taking on board some key scientists with particular skills in a highly specialised field. The transitional planning had been poor and the scientists were dissatisfied with the new operating culture. There was a risk of a mass exodus. Simon, as chief operating officer for this particular division of the company, had just held a meeting with the lead managers of both organisations to resolve what appeared to be many contentious issues. Months later, with the benefit of

(continued)

(continued)

hindsight, everyone recognised it was this meeting, organised and led by Simon that had made the difference and turned what looked like being an unmitigated disaster into an unqualified success.

Over a period of six months prior to this meeting Simon had completed a series of eight coaching sessions. The management board had put him forward for coaching as they felt his performance was not having the personal impact required for the role he had been promoted to. Simon was an excellent technician with a background in engineering and systems analysis. He had been promoted because of the outstanding contribution he had made to the company over the years. Now he was managing a division with responsibility for over 500 employees.

Simon is six foot four inches in height. Prior to coaching he walked with a pronounced stoop. His internal coach (assigned to him from the company's HR department) reported that he was considered absent-minded, with his 'head in the clouds'. He appeared to move in an uncoordinated fashion and was constantly 'knocking into things'. He spoke very quietly with a strong regional accent and his colleagues found it difficult to understand what he was saying. People also complained that he rarely made eye contact in one-to-one meetings.

This chapter considers 'performance in the workplace' and uses Simon's story to highlight and explore some of the key principles of performance from the perspective of the Feldenkrais Method.

Introduction

Performance is a word used frequently in the work place. Employees are constantly asked to consider their performance, and their performance is monitored by an increasing number of professionals trained in a variety of psychometrics, tools and techniques. Coaches are constantly asked to help improve the performance of their clients' employees, and business managers are called on to supervise the performance of their subordinates. As a result performance is a word that can have as many connotations as the people defining it.

From an etymological view the word performance is made up of the verb 'to perform' and the suffix '-ance'. 'To perform' comes from the Anglo Norman 'perfourmer', meaning to complete, finish, bring about, accomplish. The suffix 'ance' turns the verb into a noun. As it is a 'living' suffix it represents an 'action' as well as a state and condition, or quality. Definitions of performance referring to stage and theatre, i.e. 'the "action" of putting on a play', arrive much later in history. Nevertheless, both definitions suggest that action is a key element of performance. Performance can be considered as the 'action of doing something'. So when performance development is discussed it could be said that it is the 'action' of doing something we are looking to improve.

The Feldenkrais Method: the nature of action

Action is inherent within performance. Therefore, in order to develop performance there has to be an improvement in the action of whatever is being undertaken.

A key principle underpinning the Feldenkrais Method, and one that recurs throughout this book, is that every action consists of four elements: thinking, feeling (emotion), sensation, and movement. Each one of these elements will be present to some degree or another in every thing we do. In Chapter 2, Karl was extremely anxious about having to make a presentation. The feeling (emotion) associated with the anxiety had a corresponding thought, a sensation, and a postural expression (movement). Therefore, when considering the improvement of performance from the perspective of improving the action, it helps to understand what these elements actually are and how they operate and interrelate with each other.

The following is a brief description of each element from the perspective of the Feldenkrais Method.

Thinking

It is the human ability for abstraction that has resulted in our species evolving into the most effective predators and efficient scavengers on the planet. Thinking is associated with the frontal cortex. The frontal cortex was one of the later parts of the brain to evolve. It is also one of the slowest parts of the brain to mature after birth. Abstract concepts such as left and right, forward and backwards, $1 + 1 = 2$, and the ability to verbalise them, are skills that have not been developed to any great extent in other living creatures. Being able to think and talk in abstract concepts has resulted in the creation of the many professions required to live in a highly complex ordered society.

Feeling

An individual's emotional reaction to their surroundings primarily dictates their behaviour. Emotions are part of the functioning of the limbic system (sometimes known as the mammalian brain). Whilst many of the functions of the limbic system are duplicated in the other hemispheres of the brain, the basic emotional responses relating to survival, often referred to as the 'fight flight freeze' responses, are based in the amygdala. Instinctive emotional reactions are a natural response to danger and operate at a faster speed than rational thought. An individual's emotional reaction to any given situation is also often influenced by the memory of similar events. Long term memory is one of the functions of the hippocampus, which is also part of the limbic system, and operates at a speed faster than the frontal cortex which provides checks and balances on our behaviour. This is why we sometimes react (like John and Bill did in Chapter 1) without awareness of the probable outcome of our actions.

Sensation

The physical interaction we experience with the world is channelled through our five senses. With the exception of smell, all sensory information comes into the thalamus (another part of the limbic system). This information is then forwarded to other parts of the brain for processing. Sensation provides information about our relationship with the environment, including gravity. However, our awareness of sensation is often not that well developed, for example, as you read this are you aware of your feet? When you walk are you aware of the contact of your feet with the ground? Sometimes people are so identified with their thinking that they have very little awareness of what is going on around them. An individual can walk into a meeting completely unaware of how they got there. Developing awareness of sensation is a useful tool as it allows you to be aware of the present moment. In the present moment it is possible to observe our own behaviour and check our emotional reactions.

Movement

Without movement there is no life. We need muscular activity for respiration, the pumping of the heart, digestion and regulation of body temperature. We need to be able to move to find food, prepare it and eat it. We need to move to find places to rest and sleep safely. We need to be able to move in order to socially interact. These movements are controlled by the motor cortex of the brain in conjunction with the cerebellum. The cerebellum co-ordinates the learning of, and the application of complex motor skills. The majority of the nervous system is engaged in movement of one type or another. We tend to recognise an emotion from the corresponding physical movement it engages. As Moshe Feldenkrais pointed out 'most of what goes on within us remains dulled and hidden from us until it reaches the muscles'.[2]

Moshe Feldenkrais considered that the self-improvement of an individual could not generally be achieved through isolated work on one component of action alone. Effective performance requires the connection of perceptual thinking, physical presence and emotional state. However he concluded that because the majority of our nervous system is concerned with movement, the most effective way towards achieving this was by developing awareness through movement.

Performance at work

In the workplace an individual's 'overall' performance is generally measured through two categories of competence; the application of 'Technical' (hard) skills and the application of 'Behavioural' (soft) skills.

'Technical' performance relates to the practical ability to apply knowledge to physically produce something and/or undertake a practical task and complete it. For example, a nurse or doctor requires medical knowledge about the body and illness in order to assess a patients needs. They also need the practical skills, such as being able to take blood or stitch up a wound in order to treat the patient. An accountant needs both financial knowledge and the technical ability to combine figures arithmetically and then interpret them. All professions require some degree of technical ability and many organisations place substantial resources into developing these skills and setting performance measures to ensure they are being applied effectively.

However the quality of 'overall' performance in the workplace depends on an individual's ability to interact with other people. 'Behavioural' performance, sometimes referred to as the 'soft skills', is the ability to communicate thoughts and ideas to individuals or groups of people in a way that enables a practical task to be completed efficiently. 'Behavioural' performance also includes the individual's personal resilience, and ability to cope with stress.

There is little doubt that an individual's 'Technical' performance is important to most employers, however, the importance of 'Behavioural' performance is increasingly recognised and much more training is now being provided in the development of the 'soft' skills. Our personal health and wellbeing together with how successful we are in life depend on our ability to communicate effectively with one another.

Simon's managers had no issue regarding his 'Technical' performance, he had excelled in his previous role. He was promoted on the basis of his technical skills as an engineer and systems analyst. Unfortunately when they promoted him they did not consider his 'Behavioural' performance. This happens more frequently than most organisations would care to admit – the outstanding self-motivated sales executive who achieves their targets will not necessarily have the skills to become an outstanding manager of sales people.

The Feldenkrais Method is concerned with both 'Technical' and 'Behavioural' performance. In terms of the 'Technical' performance, Feldenkrais practitioners can work together with individuals and teams to help them to find more efficient and healthy ways to bring into 'action' what is required of them. However, the Feldenkrais method can also have a deep and significant effect on an individual's 'Behavioural' performance especially in relation to the development of emotional intelligence, resilience and the ability to cope with stress.

If we return to the key themes that coaches and managers are often asked to help individuals address they include: assertiveness, communication skills, emotional intelligence, innovative thinking, impact and presence, influencing skills, resilience, and work life balance. Any improvement in these areas require the development of the so called 'soft' skills associated with 'Behavioural' performance. As discussed in Chapter 1, the ability to develop these skills requires awareness.

Yet when Simon was asked what he wanted to achieve from his coaching sessions he couldn't answer. He had no awareness of how he currently performed or the effect his actions were having on the business and the people he managed. He came along to the first coaching session with an open mind but no idea about what he wanted to achieve. His performance review, which had recommended coaching, shed no light on what was wanted, it simply said 'Simon lacks a certain something that seems to impede on his management of others.' He wanted to improve his performance but had no awareness of what this would look like in practice, and neither did the people who managed him.

Simon was encouraged to answer a series of questions – how would you like to perform? How would you like your colleagues to perceive you? What type of leader would you like to be? In order to help him find an answer he was asked to consider the following statement: 'If you think about the managers that have had a positive influence on your working life, what qualities did they display that you admired most?' He came up with a list of qualities that enabled him to set very specific aims and objectives.

Within six months, his whole management style had changed for the better. He was increasingly self aware and the impact he had on others. His overall 'performance' had significantly changed. He attributed a large part of what he had achieved to the Awareness Through Movement lessons he had been encouraged to take as part of the coaching intervention.

Awareness in performance

In the sociological discipline of 'Symbolic Interactionism'[3] performance is considered as a social interaction (communication) between two or more people where each person adopts a role based on the personal (symbolic) meaning they have given to whatever is happening in the moment.

Every day a person will adopt and play out a multitude of different roles, for example, manager, work colleague, salesperson, trainer, teacher, coach, mother, father, aggrieved customer. Each role will be played out in accordance with the meaning given to it either consciously or subconsciously. Although some of these roles may feel natural, how well they are performed depends on the individual's level of awareness. Shakespeare's famous quote 'All the world's a stage. . .' certainly feels applicable as on one level, life can be observed as a performance.

In theatrical performance the successful actor/actress spends a great deal of time rehearsing the meaning of their role and how it will be communicated to the audience in a way that generates a specific reaction. In order to do this, the performer needs to be fully aware of what they are doing in relationship with the audience. The successful actor *learns* to perform with self-awareness.

In the work place outstanding managers, like Simon, *learn* to perform with self-awareness. Each performance, whether it is a meeting, presentation, or a one-to-one with a colleague, requires as much planning and rehearsal as an actor undertakes when they are learning to play out a role on stage. Whilst this may appear to be time consuming in the early stages, with experience the time required is less and the results more than compensate for the cost. The outstanding manager needs to consider what outcomes they expect as a result of their interactions with others. Performance in the work place is not something that should be left to chance, and yet it so often is. The ramifications of this were discussed in Chapter 1.

Sometimes it is assumed that high achievers are born with an innate ability to perform with poise, confidence and impact. Nevertheless all the skills they display will have been learnt and practised at some time or another. It is also sometimes assumed that because a person has reached a certain level of seniority, often because of their technical skills and knowledge, they must already have the self-awareness to perform in this manner. This was the assumption that had been made initially about Simon.

Each human being is a complex and unique individual with their own personal self-image. From the perspective of the Feldenkrais Method one of the issues impeding performance is a lack of awareness. We all need to develop our awareness; the awareness of who we are, how we currently perform, what the limitations of our performance are, and, how we would like to perform. The development of awareness, especially in the way the person relates to their working environment, has a beneficial return on investment. Awareness Through Movement lessons provide a framework for considering performance and enabling its exploration in a way that is meaningful, safe, fun and stimulating and accessible to everyone.

Awareness Through Movement lesson: dynamic sitting

This lesson in Awareness Through Movement is similar to one that Simon was given. He was concerned about his presence and impact when he had to sit through long meetings. The lesson is designed to make sitting more comfortable and at the same time assist you in being more aware of the surrounding environment. When you are sitting dynamically, you are more alert and available to respond to what is going on around you. It improves performance.

The human being was not designed for sitting – at least not for long periods of time. The ability to be alert to surroundings and to be able to move in all directions is what enabled humans to survive and evolve beyond our predecessors. Our recently-developed habit of sitting, sitting still, and added to that, keeping the eyes at a static distance on a screen in front of us, has diminished the ability to perform many of the functions which were, and are still, needed for survival. We may question if the need to avoid being eaten by a tiger is still realistic, but the basic awareness of our environment is even more important where we are sharing space with thousands of others. It also helps to be aware of our colleagues and the people we manage, especially in important meetings such as the one Simon chaired in the case story.

First of all, you will need a comfortable chair. This is a topic on which an entire chapter can be devoted, but for now, what you need is a chair where you can sit forward towards the edge and have your feet flat on the floor. Most chairs are manufactured to be a standard height and this is a supportive height for only a small percentage of human beings – and for most, the standard chair height is too high. If you cannot sit on the edge of the chair, with your feet flat on the floor, then please put something on the floor to raise the height of your feet – something sturdy that you could also stand on. You will want to be able to have an approximate 90 degree angle between your torso and your upper legs and at your knees, between your upper legs and lower legs.

Sit forward on the chair and feel the contact your feet make with the floor. So many people sit with their feet crossed, or with just the front of the feet touching the floor, not realising how important organisation of the feet and legs are to supportive sitting.

– slide your right foot forward so that your heel is no longer below your knee and your entire foot stays in contact with the floor – your knee will begin to 'unbend' and the angle in your ankle joint will become more open, then bring your foot back so that your ankle is right below your knee, returning to the 90 degree angle. Notice the muscular effort in both your lower and upper legs while doing this forward movement. Repeat several times.

Stop and rest, returning your foot so that your ankle is below your knee.

Slide your right foot back so that your heel is no longer below your knee and keep your entire foot in contact with the floor. You may find that this direction is limited compared to the forward direction; feel the bend in the knee increase and feel the decrease in the angle of the ankle joint, the lengthening of the muscles in the back of the lower leg and the shortening of the muscles in the front of the leg.

Stop and rest, returning your foot so that your ankle is below your knee.

Do the same exploration with your left foot and notice any differences between the right and the left side. Do the same exploration with both feet together.

Sit back in the chair and rest from being upright.
Sitting upright, if you are not accustomed to it, will feel like a strain. Most people sit with too much contraction in the muscles in the front of the torso or with too much contraction in the muscles in the lower back. It will take a while to learn to balance the use of these two sets of muscles, so that sitting upright will feel as though the structure of your spine is keeping you sitting and the muscles can minimise their involvement. The position of your feet play an important role in the organisation of

(continued)

(continued)

your legs in sitting, supporting being upright. This may not feel obvious at first, but it will make more sense as this lesson continues.

Sit forward on the edge of the chair again, arrange your legs so that your lower legs and upper legs are at approximate right angles.

- lift the heel of your right foot so that the weight will fall into the ball of your foot; keep it lifted and rotate the heel outwards and put the heel down; you may notice that your right knee falls inwards slightly. Repeat this a few times.
- while doing the same movement of your heel outwards, attempt to separate the movement of your foot from that of your upper leg, so that your knee remains where it was at the start and stays there while your heel is moving outwards; feel the rotation movement in your entire lower leg.

Stop and rest.

Now lift the heel of your right foot and rotate your heel inwards and put the heel down; you may notice this time that your right knee falls outwards slightly. Some people sit like this regularly as they don't know how to organise their legs in a supportive way underneath them. Feel that when your right knee falls outwards, the weight rolls on to the outside of your foot and the inner side of the foot will no longer be in contact with the floor.

- while doing this same movement of your heel inwards, keep your knee in the same place as at the start while your heel moves inwards and feel the rotational movement in your lower leg. Do this same exploration with your left foot, noticing any differences.
- slide one, or both feet back and lean forward with your entire torso and come to stand. Walk around and feel your feet on the floor, the movement in your ankles, knees and hip-joints as you walk.

Stop and rest.

Sit again on the edge of the chair.

- lift the right side of your pelvis away from the chair until you can slide your hand, palm up underneath, then let your weight come down onto your hand and you will feel your sitting bone resting in

the palm of your hand. The sitting bone, or ischial tuberosity, is the bony structure of the pelvis on which your weight falls while sitting.
- lift the right side of your pelvis again, take your hand away and let the weight of the right side of your pelvis rest on the seat of the chair again. Can you perceive this sitting bone more clearly now than the other?

Stop and rest.

Most people are not aware of their skeletal structures and how important this awareness is to finding a comfortable and more vital way of sitting. The sitting bone is designed so that it can balance the weight of the upper torso. If you sit with your weight too far back on your sitting bones, as in slouching, the muscles in the front of your torso will contract, bringing both your shoulders and your head forwards and downwards so that your torso makes a shape like the letter 'C'. Your digestive tract and breathing muscle will become contracted, interfering with these functions. So slouching is not being in a 'relaxed state', as many may feel, but it is inefficient. In order to come to stand, as in the previous step, you would need to first erect your back before you can lean forward with your entire torso. Moshe Feldenkrais described ideal posture, like this: 'you want to be able to move in all of the cardinal directions – forwards, backwards; upwards, downwards; to the right and to the left – without needing to make a preliminary re-organisation.'

If you find yourself slouching, then often when you want to erect yourself, or 'sit up straight', you roll too far forward on your sitting bones and need to strongly contract the muscles of your lower back, pushing your abdomen forward. Holding this lower back contraction creates a strain on your neck and the carriage of your head, so this is also not an efficient way to sit.

Sit on the edge of the chair again. Place your feet so that your upper and lower legs are at a 90 degree angle and feel the contact of the bottom of your feet on the floor. Find the place where you feel balanced on your sitting bones

- roll back on your sitting bones so that you feel your abdominal muscles begin to contract and your shoulders, neck and head pull downwards; your chin moves towards your chest, making a full 'C' shape with your torso; notice that the back of your torso is

(continued)

(continued)

now long, while the front shortens. If you attempt to look at a computer screen from this position, you will have to make an effort to contract the back of your neck to bring your eyes to a horizontal level.

– roll back to sit again on the top of your sitting bones. Roll backwards and return a few times so that you can clearly feel how the change in where your weight falls on your sitting bones affects the entire organisation of your torso.

Stop and rest.

Sit on the edge of the chair again.

– roll forward on your sitting bones so that you feel your lower back muscles contract and your abdomen move forwards; notice that your chin moves away from your chest and your eyes look a bit upwards. If you attempt to look at a computer screen from this position, you will have to make an effort to straighten the back of your neck to bring your eyes to the horizon.

– roll back to sit again on the top of your sitting bones. Roll forwards and return a few times so that you can clearly feel when the weight falls forward on your sitting bones, how it affects the organisation of your torso.

– roll once forwards and once backwards on your sitting bones, and then find a 'neutral' place between these two options. You will find that in this 'neutral' place, you can sit comfortably with your torso upright. Congratulations, you have just experienced one of the 'secrets' of comfortable and dynamic sitting!

Stop and rest.

While sitting, especially in front of a computer screen, the tendency is to focus straight ahead and 'forget' that there is a world to the right and to the left. It is important when spending much time looking at a screen to move your eyes from this fixed position. This will be covered more in depth in the chapter on seeing.

Sit, once again, on the front edge of the chair. From the previous explorations, you can now organise your legs and feet to support your upright sitting and you can more easily find the place on which to balance on your sitting bones.

- turn your head and eyes to the left; be sure that you are only rotating in your neck and that your shoulders are still facing to the front. Repeat this movement a few times. Notice how far you can turn easily and find something you can see in your surroundings that lines up with the tip of your nose as a way of 'measuring' how far you can turn without making extra efforts.

Stop and rest.

Turn your head and eyes again to the left and stay at the place where the range of movement is easy.

- now move both shoulders so that your right shoulder moves forward and your left shoulder moves back; you will notice that your head and eyes now rotate further to the left; note what you can see in your surroundings that lines up with the tip of your nose – by how many degrees of rotation has the range of movement increased?
- return to the middle, now turn the head, eyes, and shoulders together to the left several times.
- turn just your head and eyes to the left again, leaving your shoulders facing forward – has the range of this movement increased?

Stop and rest.

Turn your head, eyes and shoulders to the left and stay at the place where you can rotate easily. Notice if you can feel the rotational movement all the way to your right hip joint. Don't worry if you cannot.

- place the palm of your left hand on the chair near the left side of your pelvis and your right palm to rest on your right thigh, slide your right knee a bit forward so that your pelvis is now also rotating. You may need to lift the right sitting bone slightly to allow for this movement to be easy.
- rotate your pelvis and let your knee slide forward; do this several times. Notice when your pelvis begins to rotate that your head, eyes and your shoulders can rotate further – by now you might be able to look almost behind you!

(continued)

(continued)

Stop and rest.

In the story of evolution, being upright enables movement around the central axis of the spine and this is what gave early humans the ability to see the full range of the surrounding environment, enabling them to observe any possible enemies or predators from a distance and get out of the way of an attack. The range of this rotational movement is optimal when the spine is upright.

Sit at the edge of the chair – roll backwards on your sitting bones and allow your shoulders and head to fall forward; stay in this position and move your eyes, head and shoulders to the left. Notice the restriction in the range of rotation, compared to when your torso is upright.

I hope that this is convincing as to how inefficient 'slouching' can be and how detrimental it can be to your relationship to the environment.

Slide one, or both feet, a bit closer so that you can lean forward with your torso and come easily to standing. In standing, turn to the left and to the right. Notice if the range of rotational movement is further to the left than to the right.

You may want to repeat the steps starting from the one of rotating your head, now in the direction to the right, in order to balance the differences in the range of rotational movement.

Notes

1 Moshe Feldenkrais (2010). Embodied wisdom: the collected papers of Moshe Feldenkrais; edited by Elizabeth Beringer. Berkeley, CA: North Atlantic Books.
2 Moshe Feldenkrais (1990). Awareness through movement: easy to do health exercises to improve your posture, vision, imagination, and personal awareness. New York: HarperCollins.
3 Mead, George H (2015) Mind, self and society: from the viewpoint of a social behaviorist. Chicago: University of Chicago Press.

4 Learning to breathe

Most people do not use the increased vitality that can be obtained from full and regular breathing; in most cases they do not know what such breathing means.[1]

Moshe Feldenkrais

Case story

Peter is a senior change manager for a reputable consultancy firm in the City. He has worked with this firm for the last seven years and has just failed in a promotion bid to director grade. In the feedback from the panel who interviewed him it was suggested that he had appeared nervous and should consider receiving some coaching to increase his overall level of confidence. He reacted negatively to this feedback yet has agreed to be coached.

He has signed up for four sessions. During the first meeting he related his career history to date. It was an interesting story. Prior to his career in management consultancy he had been a professional tennis player. He had played at international level in competition around the world before embarking on a reputable career as a tennis coach. Minor injuries led him to cut short his sporting career and undertake an MBA with a prestigious business school. He had then moved into consultancy specialising in change management. It was immediately apparent that Peter did not have a personal confidence issue.

(continued)

(continued)

However, as he spoke it was impossible not to notice that he was continually breathing through his mouth. He did not breathe through his nose at all, even when he was not speaking. This was having an impact, albeit a minor one, on his speech. He appeared to be breathless, gasping for air at the end of a sentence at which point the volume of his voice would decrease noticeably. At other times he would finish a sentence with an audible exhalation of breath followed by an equally audible inhalation of air.

The way he was breathing gave visual and auditory cues that many of us sub-consciously interpret as a person being nervous or anxious. When we are nervous and anxious we have a tendency to breathe through the mouth. Because we make sense of others' experience through the lens of our own it was hardly surprising that the interview panel assumed he was nervous. Yet, in this case, it was obvious from Peter's other behaviours, the way he moved, the words he spoke, that he was completely at ease with his surroundings.

Why we breathe

Breathing as a biological function is so natural to us that we rarely stop to consider it. Obviously we all have to breathe in order to live. However, the efficiency of our breathing is so vital to our health, well-being and state of mind that it is worth taking the time to explore the mechanics and how inefficiencies within the biological process are often an underlying contributor to ill-health and poor performance in the work place.

We inhale air to take in a vital form of nourishment – oxygen. We exhale to expel waste matter – principally carbon dioxide. Once we are born, breathing is the only way to supply our body and its various organs with the oxygen required for survival. The actual biological process is under the subconscious autonomous control of the brain stem. Whilst we can consciously control our breathing, which we do primarily when we speak or purposely hold our breath, we cannot stop ourselves from breathing. The mechanism is regulated by the levels of carbon dioxide in the blood. Once this exceeds a certain level an instinctive reaction generated by the brain stem compels us to take a breath.

Oxygen is essential for the maintenance of the brain, nerves, glands and internal organs. We can do without food for weeks and without water for days, but without oxygen, we will die within a few minutes.

When we are at rest we normally take 12 to 18 breaths per minute; this is our resting breathing rate. In exercise or when we are our nervous and anxious the breathing rate may increase, and, in meditation or deep relaxation the breathing rate may reduce. However, in general, a breathing rate consistently outside the 12 to 18 cycle would be considered abnormal.

The brain requires three times more oxygen than any other part of the body. If it doesn't get enough, the result is mental sluggishness, negative thoughts and depression, followed eventually with a decline in vision and hearing. Without oxygen brain cells start dying within four minutes. Lack of oxygen in the heart causes coronaries. Lack of oxygen to the brain causes strokes. Oxygen is essential for healthy living and for effective performance in all aspects of our lives regardless of profession.

The amount of air we introduce to our lungs is important for effective speech. The quality and the volume of the sound made is dependent on the amount of breath we have available to expel. The amount we have available to expel is in a direct ratio to the amount of air we have inhaled. Consequently we need to fully utilise our lung capacity and learn to control our breathing when speaking. If the breathing is ineffective the meaning of our communication may get lost as others are detracted from our performance. This is primarily what had happened to Peter during his interview.

Nasal versus oral breathing

The healthiest way to breathe in is through the nose; it moistens and warms the air. Hairs inside the nostrils trap pollutants such as dust particles and most germs. Breathing out through the nose allows moisture to be re-absorbed by the same hairs thereby reducing the risk of dehydration.

Breathing through the mouth often encourages upper chest breathing and poor use of the diaphragm. Mouth breathers have lower levels of oxygen in their blood. Air that hasn't been filtered through the nose can damage the lungs. It also allows irritants to get onto the vocal folds. Breathing through the mouth dries out the oral cavity. This encourages increased acidity in the mouth and can lead to dental problems and gum disease.[2,3] Take a moment to experience the difference between the two forms of breathing – take four breaths in through the mouth and then four through the nose.

Whilst there is no question that habitual breathing through the mouth is not the healthiest way to breathe, occasionally most of us will, especially when we are nervous and anxious or undertaking physical activity. This is why some people get a dry mouth when they have to present. The anxiety they have about presenting causes them to breathe through the mouth. Whilst there may be occasions where breathing through the mouth is necessary, it is generally inefficient and occasionally dangerous. Whilst the following story is somewhat extreme it does highlight the risks.

This tale was told by an actor several years ago during one of the regular Voice Clinic days held by the British Voice Association[4]. He was playing Hamlet at Regents Park Open Air Theatre. As he was taking a breath through his mouth prior to commencing a speech he took in a sycamore seed that went down his trachea (wind pipe) towards the lungs. As he choked, the seed was discharged injuring both his vocal and vestibular folds. These fibroelastic ligaments are responsible for creating a seal that normally prevents foreign object from entering the lungs when we swallow, but lie open when we breathe (see Chapter 8 – Learning to talk). Consequently the ligaments swelled up preventing air from entering the trachea and into the lungs. As a result he couldn't breathe and required an emergency tracheotomy.

Breathing and emotion

At any given time our breathing pattern is closely related to what we are feeling and it will change according to our moods, often without us realising it.

When we experience high levels of stress or anxiety the brain sends signals, resulting in the release of the hormones cortisol and adrenaline. This raises the breathing and heart rate to encourage the body to convert fat into glucose thereby producing the physical energy required to deal with the situation. This is natural and normal. However, the flow of blood and oxygen is directed primarily to the muscles away from the other key organs in the body, including the brain and in particular the pre-frontal cortex, the area responsible for rational thinking.

Even a slight change in the level of oxygen to the brain alters the way a person thinks, feels and behaves. Stress, anxiety and fear affect people in different ways, however the reduction of oxygen to the brain can make the individual more impulsive, confused and prone to behaviour that may be considered by others as negative and aggressive.

The tendency towards shallow breathing

Most of us do not breathe as efficiently as we could and this may impede on our personal health and well-being. Changes in lifestyles over the past 40 years and the move towards sedentary jobs are factors associated with the increase in certain breathing disorders and lung diseases. The types of poor posture that can result from sitting at a desk can lead to inefficiencies in breathing – the two are closely linked. As indicated above inefficient breathing reduces the individual's capacity to think and solve problems. Low oxygen levels in the body also leads to fatigue.

The total capacity of the lungs is between 4 to 6 litres depending on a person's age and size. In a 'normal' breath an individual will take in around .3 to .5 litres. The volume of air that can actually exchange in a deep breath is between 3 to 5 litres. Approximately 1 litre of residual air always remains in the lungs to keep them partially inflated. Most individuals will rarely use their lungs to their full capacity. It is believed that most of us now only use our lungs to between ten to thirty per cent of their natural capacity. Consequently this results in many of us experiencing the health and wellbeing issues discussed above.

The key reasons that lead to a degeneration in breathing are:

- The increased stress and pace of modern living. This results in increasing the rate of our breathing cycle resulting in a shallower intake of air;
- The introduction of technology and the sedentary nature of many professions. The lack of physical activity required in our work means there is less need to breathe deeply. Shallower forms of breathing and poor posture at the desk become habitual;
- More people are spending their life working indoors where the air is less fresh. Air quality in office spaces can often be poor especially in built up areas. Not only are there the outdoor contaminants coming through ventilation systems but also internal emissions that arise from: office technology; building materials; fabrics and furnishings; cleaning chemicals. In these situations breathing patterns may become shallower in order to limit the intake of pollutants.

The first thing anyone can do to improve their breathing, especially if they are employed in a sedentary job, is to take regular breaks. Moving around, laughing and talking will readjust your posture and will ease a constricted breathing pattern. Get up from your desk every twenty minutes and take a quick walk around the office. If employers could develop environments that allow for healthy, wholesome breathing much would be done to improve overall performance and wellbeing in the workplace.

The anatomy of breathing

Breathing is a complex process engaging many parts of the body. What follows is a basic approximation of the breathing process and more details are included within the Awareness Through Movement lesson at the end of this chapter.

We have two lungs, left and right, housed within the ribcage. The right lung is larger than the left and is divided into three lobes and the bronchial tube continuing from the trachea (wind pipe), divides into three branches.

The left lung is smaller as it shares the space it inhabits with the heart. It is divided into two lobes with the bronchial tube divided into two branches. The lungs themselves are inert. The outer lining of the lungs – the pleura – is attached to the ribs and the diaphragm. The diaphragm is a dome-like sheaf of muscles separating the upper and lower parts of the torso. The diaphragm is attached to the lower parts of the ribs going up to the base of the sternum. The three main origins of the diaphragm are on the xiphoid process of the sternum, the deep surfaces of the 7–12 ribs and parts of the 1–3 lumbar vertebrae. In between the ribs are the muscles known as the intercostals.

When we breathe in the diaphragm muscle fibres flatten, moving downwards, expanding the lower ribs. At the same time the shoulder and collarbone lift allowing the upper ribs to expand. This increases the cavity of the ribcage and as the lungs are attached to all the component parts they expand the fill the space, drawing air in through the nose, past the palate, through the larynx, into the trachea, through the bronchial tubes and into the lungs.

Recognising different breathing patterns

Unless we have learnt how to breathe effectively, most of us will use a combination of three different types of habitual breathing patterns.

High Breathing (sometimes known as clavicular breathing)

High breathing takes place primarily in the upper part of the chest and lungs and involves raising the ribs, sternum, shoulder and collarbone. This is the shallow breathing associated with nervousness, anxiety, and fear. There is very little movement in the ribs downwards, forwards or backwards. The belly may be pulled inwards.

Because many people have little awareness of how to breathe, when asked to breathe deeply, you will often see them pull in their belly and take a big high breath. If the belly is drawn inwards the diaphragm muscle fibres are not flattening and the full capacity of the lungs is not utilised. This type of breathing is sometimes referred to as paradoxical breathing.

High breathing is the least effective form of breathing. It also requires more muscular effort than more efficient forms of breathing.

Low breathing (sometimes known as breathing from the stomach or diaphragm)

Low breathing takes place in the lower part of the chest and lungs. It tends to be more effective than high breathing as there is a greater intake of air.

When low breathing occurs the diaphragm flattens, pulling the ribs downwards and outwards and pushing the belly somewhat forward. The belly moves out when we breathe in and moves in when we breathe out. The western obsession with having a flat abdomen, and for holding in the belly, results in many people not allowing their diaphragm to function effectively. Low breathing occurs naturally when we sleep and often when sitting. Sedentary people who habitually bend forward while they read or write have a tendency towards low breathing. This form of breathing is sometimes associated with depression.

It is also, generally, an ineffective way to breathe when undertaking any form of physical exercise. However, it is preferable to high breathing because:

- more air is taken in when inhaling, due to greater expansion of the lungs and the fact that the lower lobes are situated in an area of the chest where there is a larger capacity.
- the movement of the diaphragm expands the base of the lungs, allowing them to draw in a larger supply of blood for the transfer of gases. This improves circulation throughout the body.
- the abdominal organs are massaged by the up and down movements of the diaphragm and this aids digestion.

Middle breathing (sometimes known as intercostal or rib breathing)

As the name suggests middle breathing exhibits some of the characteristics of both high and low breathing. The ribs rise and the chest expands and the diaphragm moves up and down. However none of the movements are sufficient to fill the lungs fully and it is therefore another form of shallow breathing. It is less effective than low breathing but more effective than high breathing.

Efficient breathing

There may, of course, be other reasons why a person does not breathe efficiently. Peter's case is interesting in this regard.

When asked about his breathing Peter looked puzzled. He had always breathed through his mouth and considered that it was the normal way to do so. He was surprised to learn that the most natural, safe and effective way to breathe was through his nose. As he told his story it transpired that he had developed nasal polyps as a child and couldn't breathe through his nose. Consequently he had to breathe through his mouth. This way of breathing became 'natural' to him, so even after the polyps had been removed he continued to breathe in this way. What had been an essential habit for a temporary period of time became a permanent behaviour.

Peter was given a variety of lessons focussing on breathing. The following year Peter was promoted to director.

Awareness Through Movement lesson: exploring breathing

Many people do not believe they can improve the way they breathe or increase their lung capacity. Generally the act of breathing is an involuntary reflex action controlled by the medulla oblongata (the older part of the brain). However, when we breathe consciously or try and control our breathing, the neo-cortex (the latest part of the brain to evolve) takes responsibility for most of the process.

There are many ways in which we can explore breathing. This lesson is easiest to experience lying on your back with your knees bent. However, you could also do it in sitting with support behind you so that you can sit upright without strain.

This simple breathing lesson will be useful in many ways. If you are about to give a talk, or have an important discussion, doing some of these explorations beforehand will organise your breathing to support your speaking voice. If you become nervous and want to alter your state, recall some of the steps of this lesson. This lesson can also be useful if you are experiencing the signs of an approaching cold or respiratory disturbance. If you have any asthmatic tendencies, use this lesson to find out if it can make a difference. And if you find yourself feeling fatigued, this lesson can give you a boost in alertness.

Take in a deep breath and let it out. Notice what areas of your torso you move while taking in air. Where is the largest expansion – in the upper or lower part of your chest? Notice if you contract any of your back muscles while breathing in.

When you contract your back muscles, they shorten and this can give the impression of being more upright. The muscles in the front of the torso are often chronically shortened, which produces a slight flexion; when the flexion increases, this is what is known as 'slouching'. Contracting and thereby shortening the back muscles produces a forward curve of the spine which allows the front of the chest to lengthen, giving a contrast to the flexion, and a feeling of being upright. But it is an illusion to think that this creates more space for the movement of the breath. It actually narrows the space between the spine and the ribcage in the upper chest and pushes the abdomen forward in the lower chest. If you find yourself contracting your back muscles as you take in a deep breath, it inhibits the movements which expands the back of the chest; thereby decreasing the volume of air that can be taken in.

If you are lying on your back, keep your entire back in contact with the floor while taking a deep breath in and at the same time, feel your sternum (breastbone) moving away from your spine. If you are sitting, while taking in a deep breath, you can lengthen your entire back and keep it in contact with the support, or you can even press slightly against the support, again while feeling the sternum moving forward and, at the same time, your upper torso moving slightly back. Awareness of the movement/expansion of the torso in all 360 degrees of its round shape will bring about more efficient breathing.

The ribcage is constructed to respond to the expansion and contraction of the lungs. The sternum is composed partly of cartilage, as are the connections of the ribs to the sternum. Cartilage is not as solid as is bone and it has some degree of movement. The bottom two ribs are not even attached to the chest in the front, allowing for the largest amount of expansion as they are situated closest to the breathing muscle, the diaphragm.

Take in a more normal breath and pay attention to the sensation of the air coming in both nostrils, how it brushes the back of your throat, then reaches your windpipe, or trachea. Does the air pass through each nostril equally?

–   place your right index finger to close your right nostril and notice how the air comes in and out of your left nostril. Take 2–3 breaths while observing this.
–   now do the same with your left index finger closing your left nostril and notice how the air enters your right one. Are they different? Is one easier to breathe through?

Stop and rest.

Close the nostril that you found more difficult to breathe through. Take a deep breath in and as you breathe out through that nostril make a low, rumbling sound and feel the vibration in the soft tissue of the

(continued)

(continued)

nostril. Continue making this sound until the end of the out-breath. Breathe normally for 1–2 breathing cycles, then repeat this a few times. Now close the same nostril again and breathe in normally – does that nostril feel even wider?

Close the nostril that you found easier to breathe through. Take a deep breath in and as you breathe out through that nostril, make a low, rumbling sound, continuing it to the finish of the out-breath. Breathe normally for 1–2 breathing cycles, then repeat this a few times. Now close the same nostril again and breathe in normally – does it feel clearer to breathe through this less easy nostril now?

Stop and rest.

There are two lungs, one on the right, which has three branches, called bronchi; the left lung has to share space with the heart and a part of the stomach and only has two branches. The lungs themselves are not solid and are more like a thick liquid which expands into any empty space. They are enveloped by a strong membrane, which is connected to the walls of the chest.

Getting to know the right lung

Take a full breath in and feel the movement at the bottom of the right lung – how it expands downwards, side-wards and backwards. Each time you breathe in, focus on this right, lower bronchus. If you place your right hand on your lower right ribs, you will feel the movement of the lower ribs, especially the lower two ribs which are called 'floating' ribs; as you may recall, these are not connected to the ribcage in the front.

–   repeat taking in a full breath about three times, giving time to discover how you can direct the movement of your in breath in all directions in this lower right area, corresponding to the lower right bronchus.

Stop and rest.

Take a full breath in and this time, feel the movement of the upper part of the right lung; you will feel the upper ribs expanding, the collarbone rising and a small movement of the right shoulder blade; again this expansion can be felt upwards, side-wards and backwards.

Stop and rest.

Take a full breath in and this time feel the right upper bronchus expanding upwards and at the same time, feel the right lower bronchus expanding downwards, so that the entire right side lengthens, creating the feeling of increasing the distance between the armpit and the top of the pelvis.

Stop and rest.

Take a full breath in and feel the right side lengthening as the upper bronchus expands upwards and the lower bronchus expands downwards and this time feel the middle bronchus, expanding to fill the space between the upper and lower one.

- place your left hand on top of your head, slowly tilt your head to the left (you will slide it if you are lying on your back) so that your left ear comes closer to your left shoulder. Stay like this and continue to breathe.
- with the in breath feel the three right bronchi of your lung lengthening upwards, downwards and side-wards, allowing your left ear to move slightly closer to your left shoulder and with the out-breath, allowing the head to move or slide back slightly towards the right as the right side returns to its more normal length. Repeat this about three times. The movement of your spine curving slightly more to the left as you breathe in and returning a bit as you breathe out, is a reflection of the movement of the right lung filling and emptying. Repeat this movement a number of times.

Stop and rest, then slowly stand up. Walk around and feel the difference between your right and left sides. Isn't it amazing that, just by placing your awareness in these different parts of your lungs, the sensation of the length of the two sides can be affected? Perhaps you also feel your sense of balance has altered and that you are stepping differently on your right foot than on your left?

(continued)

(continued)

This is a simple illustration of the power of awareness and of placing attention. We would usually think that it would be necessary to stretch the muscles repeatedly on one side in order to feel a similar difference.

You may feel a bit off-balance, so please lie or sit again.

Exploring the left lung

This time, as you take in a full breath, feel the movement at the bottom of the left lung – how it expands downwards, side-wards and backwards. Each time you breathe in, focus on this left, lower bronchus. You can place your left hand on your lower left ribs, feeling the movement of the lower ribs, especially the two lower 'floating' ribs. Repeat this about three times, each time finding more of the roundness of the space at the bottom of your left lung.

Stop and rest.

Breathe in again fully and this time, feel the movement of the upper part of the left lung; feel the upper ribs expanding, upwards, side-wards and to the back. Notice your collarbone rising and a small movement of the left shoulder blade, slightly rising and sinking with the in and out-breaths. Do this about three times.

Stop and rest.

Take a full breath in and feel the left side lengthening as the upper bronchus expands upwards and the lower bronchus expands downwards.

- place your right hand on top of your head, slowly tilt your head to the right (you will slide it if you are lying on your back) so that your right ear comes closer to your right shoulder. Stay like this and continue to breathe.
- with the in breath feel the bronchi of your left lung lengthening upwards, downwards and side-wards, allow your right ear to move slightly closer to your right shoulder. With the out-breath, feel that your head moves, or slides, back slightly towards the left as the

left side returns to its more normal length. Repeat this about three times. Feel the movement of your spine curving slightly more to the right as you breathe in and returning a bit as you breathe out, reflecting the movement of the air in and out of your left lung.

Stop and rest, then stand up and walk around again. Notice if your right and left sides are more alike now.

Notes

1 Moshe Feldenkrais (1990). *Awareness through movement: easy to do health exercises to improve your posture, vision, imagination, and personal awareness.* New York: HarperCollins.
2 Swift, Campbell, McKown (1988). Nasal breathing (as opposed to mouth breathing) increases circulation, blood oxygen and carbon dioxide levels, slows the breathing rate and improves overall lung volumes. Oronasal obstruction, lung volumes, and arterial oxygenation. *Lancet.* 1:73–75.
3 Elad, Wolf, and Tillman, Keck(2008). Air-conditioning in the human nasal cavity. *Respiratory Physiology & Neurobiology.*163:121–127.
4 For more information about the British Voice Association see www.britishvoice association.org.uk

5 Learning to see

The only thing permanent about our behaviour patterns is our belief that they are so.[1]

Moshe Feldenkrais

Case story

'I spent hours and hours on that report. I have hardly moved from my desk for the last month. I am exhausted, my back aches, I have a permanent headache, I feel tense all the time, and now they can't even bring themselves to acknowledge the work I have done. It has all been a waste of time.'

Chrissie is the operations director for a medium-sized business. She has been working with the firm for the last twelve months. She was brought in because the company was experiencing financial difficulties and she has been charged with developing a rescue plan. She has just presented her final report to the senior management team.

'I was so nervous because the viability of the business depends on the board taking on my recommendations. I looked at the chairman and chief executive throughout the presentation and it was impossible to see what they were thinking, and then to wrap it all up as I was explaining one of my key recommendations, they started whispering to each other. It felt like they were not paying any attention to what I was saying. They didn't even ask me any questions.'

Chrissie has been working on this presentation for some time and it was important for it to go well. From a business point of view her proposals made sense and were the logical way forward for the company. Some of the recommendations were radical but she had previously tested them out with the board who had not appeared averse to them at the time.

When Chrissie was asked about how the other members of the board had reacted to her presentation she couldn't recall even looking at them – her vision had been solely focussed on the chairman and chief executive. She assumed that everyone else's attitude was the same as they hadn't asked any questions. Obviously she was making assumptions about what everyone was thinking. As discussed in Chapter 2, her interpretation of what had happened at the meeting was partly to do with how she felt about herself at the time. She had made assumptions based on her own interpretation of the world at that moment. This was adversely affected by the hours she had spent working in the office which had taken their toll on her otherwise acute mental ability and productivity.

This story allows us to explore the nature of sight and healthy vision in the work place. The way she had been working and in particular her extensive use of digital screen equipment (smart phone, tablet, laptop and office computer) had a detrimental effect on her health. She was suffering from what is now often referred to as 'Computer Vision Syndrome'. She was displaying the typical symptoms associated with this form of repetitive strain injury – aching eyes, dry eyes, blurred vision, headache, pain in shoulder, neck and back, and anxiety. It was this that had impacted on her mental ability and productivity. It is thought that 90 per cent of people who spend three hours or more looking at computer screens without taking suitable breaks will develop the syndrome[2].

Introduction

So let us return to the premise that every action always consists of thinking, feeling (emotion), sensation, and movement. Everything we say and do is an action. Every decision made is an action. All of individual learning is through action. Every movement a person makes is an action. As human beings we are constantly in a state of action. So if we consider that 80–85 per cent of all our actions are mediated through our eyes we can appreciate just how important sight and vision is to our lives and in particular to our working lives[3].

For the majority of people who do not suffer from visual impairment it is probably fair to say that sight is often taken for granted. Yet out of the five senses it is the eyes through which a person predominantly engages with their surroundings. It is so significant that a whole section of the cerebral cortex, the occipital region, is dedicated to this function.

Sight and movement

Sight is the most complex sensory system in the body and the least developed at birth. A baby is not born with all the visual abilities needed for life. The most mature of the senses at birth is hearing.

It takes around a year for sight to develop. During the first three months the baby will start learning to focus the eyes. This is achieved by the baby paying attention to the face of the person feeding her/him. It is during this period that eye to hand co-ordination begins to develop. Initially the baby cannot move her/his eyes independently of the head so to begin they have to move their head in order to see around them.

Over the months the baby will learn to use the eyes to control movement. At the age of five months, as the child starts to learn to crawl, he/she will start to develop three dimensional vision and begin to sense distances. Early walkers may not learn to co-ordinate their eyes as well as the child who spends a little longer in the crawling stage of early development[4].

Sight and movement are intrinsically linked. Nearly all of a baby's early movements are learnt as a result of wanting to reach something they can see. The baby will explore its own body. The baby will see her/his foot and move to touch it learning that she/he has a foot. We all go through the same developmental movements – playing with our legs, learning to roll, learning to turn onto our stomach, learning to crawl, learning to walk. For the majority of us who can see, all of these movements are initiated through sight. We are naturally curious about what we observe, and it is this curiosity that develops our awareness and our self-image.

All sentient movement is initiated and organised by our eyes. Constant messages are being relayed– adjusting the size of a step we are taking in order to step over a street kerb – to change direction to avoid an obstacle we have seen. We can continue to learn and refine our movements throughout the whole of our life. However, we need to see the movement, and visualise ourselves undertaking the movement, in order to bring it into reality. The following is a simplified example of how sight works.

I have been asked by a colleague to observe her making a presentation. The room has been set up with the chairs placed in rows, theatre style, in front of the stage. I see a seat on the back row next to the door which is approximately in the centre of the wall. It gives me a clear view of centre stage and I have calculated that the distance between us will be close enough for me to observe without distracting her. I also want to sit at the back so that I do not disturb the attendees with my note taking.

She walks on to the stage. A visual stimulus of light and colour is received through my eyes. Both my eyes send this information through the optic nerve to the occipital (visual) cortex at the back of the brain for analysis. Each eye sends what is perceived at the left side of each retina to the left side of the cortex and what is sees on the right side to the right. Where the optic nerves cross over a sense of depth is created so that I can judge how far away she is from me.

I interpret what I see through my visual memory, a complex association of previous visual memories created from things I have seen in the past related to what I am seeing in the present moment. This enables me to recognise my colleague and see that she has cut her hair short since I last saw her. As I observe her I transfer information to my pre-frontal cortex for analysis.

I decide to write some notes, and using the same process that I have just used in my observations, I subconsciously visualise the movement required to operate my pen, then, almost instantaneously, I place the point of the pen on the section of note paper I have chosen to write on and start to create the words the shape of which my visual memory will convert into language when I come to read them later.

Healthy sight

'You could tell something was wrong with him; you could see it in his eyes, something not quite right.' 'Did you see her eyes? They were so bright – so alive!' On an anecdotal level many of us will have heard very similar comments. A person's overall health has often been linked to the perceived quality of the eyes. If they are 'bright' and 'alert' the person appears healthy. If they look 'dull' and 'unfocussed' the opposite is assumed. Not only do people sub-consciously make decisions about our health from the quality of our eyes, they will also make assumptions about our intelligence and motivation to work. How accurate these assumptions are could well be the subject of debate, however, there may be a degree of correlation.

Vision is important for effective performance and for emotional well-being as well. However, the way individuals work, their working environments, the way modern technology is utilised, are often not conducive to maintaining healthy vision. The health of our eyes is integral to our overall physical health and emotional wellbeing. But what constitutes healthy vision?

In the West the health of an individual's vision is often measured through the ability to read. For many years the majority of eye tests were undertaken through the assessment of a person's ability to read letters on a wall chart. More recently, however, modern technology has significantly changed the efficiency of what optometrists perceive when a person has a sight test. For example, they now use digital retinal cameras that can also detect diabetes, hypertension and other heart problems, cancers of the eye, brain tumours, and high cholesterol. However, it is still the case that most people consider themselves to have fully functional and healthy eyes provided they can see clearly and do not appear to be having problems with their vision.

Healthy vision in the workplace

The way in which people use display screen equipment in the work place is of concern – so much so that it has been the subject of a great deal of research.[5] Whilst the use of such equipment doesn't appear to have long term health issues, the numbers of users reporting symptoms of computer vision syndrome are high and probably contribute to the large percentage of days lost through anxiety and muscular skeletal disorders. In addition people suffering from the symptoms of computer vision syndrome whilst working are more likely to be less productive.

The syndrome can present varying combinations of the following – aching eyes, dry eyes, blurred vision, headache, chronic fatigue, pain in shoulder, neck and back, distress and anxiety.

Viewing a display screen is completely different from reading a printed page. On a screen letters are not so sharply delineated and there are visual difficulties caused by contrast, flicker and glare. The eyes have to work much harder, continually focussing and re-focusing as the person looks across the screen. The eye movements required place additional demands over and above those required for reading printed documents.

The viewing distance and the angle of the screen are different from those usually adopted for reading or writing. The potential problems are exacerbated if you need glasses or contact lenses. The optic nerve is surrounded by connective tissue and blood vessels. These coverings travel through the brain and eventually make a connection with the second neck vertebrae. Eye strain places the unnecessary tensions on this connective tissue that then results in neck pain. This often leads to the muscular skeletal disorders in the upper limbs that many people complain off. Obviously poor posture when sitting at the desk also plays a role. The consensus of advice given by optometrists is that the ideal setting for a screen is between 3 to 5 inches below the level of the eyes.

Generally people are at a greater risk of acquiring computer vision syndrome if they use digital screens continuously for over two hours or have to work at a screen every day.

Of increasing concern is the way in which we view one particular form of technology – the mobile phone. There is a condition which is being referred to as text neck. It is a serious condition which is beginning to affect millions of people around the world.

The condition is caused by people 'dropping' their head forward by bending over their phones (or tablets) for long periods of time. The repeated stress of this forward head flexion while looking down places extra pressure on the cervical spine. Our head weighs between 10lb and 12lb, the weight on the neck can increase to 27lbs at a 15 degree angle and 60lb at 60 degrees. This creates changes in the cervical spine moving the curvature backwards rather than forwards. The symptoms are very similar to those associated with computer vision syndrome with the potential for some additional long term health issues resulting from the increasing stress placed on the muscular skeletal system. These include: spinal degeneration; early onset of arthritis; reduction in lung capacity; disc compressions; and disc herniation.

One of the other effects that Computer Vision Syndrome and 'text neck' has relates to efficiency of eye movement. Many people now have increased difficulty moving their eyes from left to right, up and down. They can only change the direction of their eyes by moving their whole head – exactly how babies do in their early days. It could be argued that our inability to use technology effectively is making us less human – losing essential skills we gained as a species to protect ourselves from predators. We are at risk of losing peripheral vision.

Shortly after Chrissie's meeting she reviewed the way in which she had been working for the six months prior to the presentation. She had been spending over three hours a day at her laptop without taking a break. In between she was constantly texting other people in the business. She was working over sixty hours a week predominantly using digital screen devices without taking regular breaks.

Peripheral vision

It is peripheral vision that enables a person to see and be aware what is to the right and left of them whilst looking straight ahead; for example, to perceive a car coming around a bend as they are looking towards the opposite side of the road. In certain disciplines this awareness and the ability to consciously use peripheral vision is essential for success. For example, in football the players need to be able to focus on the ball, the direction of play, and be aware of everything going on around them. This enables them to perceive where their team mates are on the pitch and pass the ball with incredible accuracy. Peripheral vision of this standard is also useful in the workplace. It enables people to be able to 'read the room' and see exactly what is occurring. However, it is a skill which is often ignored and one which readily deteriorates from a lack of use. It is possible that Chrissie's inability to notice other members of the board whilst she was presenting her recommendations was the result of a deterioration in her peripheral vision.

Awareness Through Movement lesson: exploring vision

Whilst this lesson is of benefit to everyone, it is of particular benefit to those people, who like Chrissy, spend a great deal of time working with electronic screen devices. It helps 'restore' peripheral vision.

Starting in a sitting position, sit forward on a chair so that your torso can be upright, with your head balanced comfortably on the top of your spine. Close your eyes and slowly rotate your head to the right. Keep your shoulders facing forward, so that this movement takes place only in the part of the spine we know as the neck. Stop at the point where you would have to make an effort in order to turn further. Repeat this turning movement a few times.

– turn to the right again and stay where you can turn to easily. Now open your eyes and notice something vertical that you can see straight ahead of you, or extend an imaginary line from the tip of your nose and notice where it 'lands' on the wall in front of you. Remember this point.

Stop and rest.

In the same starting position, close your eyes and move only your eyes to the right and return to 'looking' straight in front of you. Do this several times, slowly, noticing if the movement of your eyes is smooth or if and where the movement 'jumps'. Notice if the movement of your eyes to the right is along a horizontal line, or if there is a slight movement upwards or downwards. Can you feel any corresponding sensations in the muscles of your neck as you repeat this movement of your eyes to the right?

Stop and rest.

With your eyes closed, move your head to the right again, going as far as it is now easy; stay there and open your eyes and notice if where you can see now is at the same vertical as in the first step or if where the imaginary line from the tip of your nose 'lands' is further along. Have you found the rotation to the right is further without making a conscious effort to rotate more?

With your eyes closed again, turn your head to the right, then also to the left and feel whether the movement to the right is different than that to the left.

Stop and rest. This time, rub the palms of your hands together until you feel them getting warm. Place the base of your palms on your cheekbones just under your eyes, place the fingers of one hand on top of the other on your forehead so that you can create a warm, dark space without putting any pressure on the eyes themselves. If you are at a desk or a table, you can rest your elbow on the table. Stay like this, for as long as you wish. You will notice the amount of this space which is actually dark and where there are sensations of light, although your hands are stopping any external light from being perceived. You may want to repeat this during any of the rests throughout the remainder of the lesson.

Following something with your eyes is the prime motivator to move your head. Using your intrinsic eye muscles, you can move your eyes all the way to the inner and outer corners of your eyes; then, in order to look further around, you have to begin to rotate your head and neck as well. When you 'fix' your eyes on a screen for long periods of time, the eyes muscles become tired from remaining in this fixed position. It is difficult to feel the effort of holding a contraction in the eye muscles, but if you contract the muscles of your hand and attempt to stay in a tight fist, you will feel the point at which the muscles tire. Remaining in a continual contraction, any muscle tires and with the eye muscles, they will gradually become weak and vision correction will be needed.

Close your eyes again and turn your head to the left; do this a few times, then stay at the point you can reach easily, open your eyes and notice something vertical or a point on the wall which would be an extension of a line from the tip of your nose and remember this line or point.

Stop and rest.

With your eyes closed, move just your eyes to the left, bringing the right eye into the inside corner of the right eye and the left eye to the outside corner of the left eye. Do this several times and notice if the line along which your eyes are moving is horizontal or if your eyes move slightly upwards or downwards and if the movement along the horizon is smooth or jumpy in places.

(continued)

(continued)

Stop and rest.

Close both eyes again; turn your head to the left and stop at the point you can move to easily. When you open your eyes, are you looking at the same vertical or point on the wall? Have you rotated further to the left without intentionally trying to do so?

Stop and rest.

Close your eyes and now turn your head to the right, stopping before you need to make an effort to turn further. Open your eyes and note again where you can see when looking straight ahead. Find a vertical element or point where you can see, extending an imaginary line from the point of your nose to the wall.

–   return to the middle again. This time, keep your eyes open and focused straight ahead and turn your head to the right. You may find it challenging to separate your eyes from the movement of your head as they both normally turn together. Notice if you find yourself holding your breath while trying to keep the eyes from moving. Repeat this movement a few times.

Stop and rest.

Close your eyes and turn both your head and your eyes, stopping at the 'border' of the easy amount of movement. Now open your eyes and notice if the point which you see straight ahead has moved a bit further to the right.

When we do an unusual movement, like this one, the habitual use of the eyes and the head is challenged. Keeping the eyes focused straight ahead while turning the head is called a 'differentiated' movement, as the eyes and head usually move together. Any 'differentiated' movement requires the breaking up of a habit, which engages higher cortical parts of the brain. It feels difficult at first, then becomes easier as the neural pathways are clarified through the repetition. The reward for this is that it 'frees up' a habitual pattern and creates, or reminds us, of new choices and possibilities.

Close your eyes and turn your head to the left, stopping just before you would need to make an effort to turn further. Open your eyes and find a point along the horizon that you can see while looking straight ahead.

– return to the middle again. Keeping your eyes open, focus on a point straight ahead and begin to turn your head to the left while your eyes remain focused straight ahead. Repeat this several times, keeping the movement light and without any strain.

Stop and rest.

Close your eyes, turn both your head and your eyes to the left. Open your eyes and notice if where you can see straight ahead is also now a little further along to the left.

It may seem a strange phenomenon that making these differentiations of the movement of your eyes and the turning of your head can result in being able to turn your head further in this rotational movement without having made a concerted effort to do so. And it may feel like a contradiction to the way many of us have been encouraged to improve the range of a movement, by effort and 'pushing' to go further. Perhaps our brains learn to increase a range of movement through becoming 'smarter, rather than working harder'.

So far you have limited the turning movement to that which can take place in the seven cervical vertebrae comprising your neck. If you recall the movements have all been done, as you were asked at the beginning, keeping your shoulders facing forwards. The amount of rotational movement in your neck is limited and whatever additional movement you now have will most probably been achieved from the steps undertaken in the lesson so far.

Sit upright again. This time, place the palms of your hands on your upper legs, near to your knees. Keep both your head facing and your eyes looking straight ahead and move both shoulders so that your left shoulder comes forward and the right moves a bit back. Do this a number of times, slowly and softly, without disturbing the 'fixed' position of your head and eyes. You will feel a rotational movement in your upper back, particularly in the area in between your shoulder blades.

Stop and rest.

Now, keeping your eyes open, turn your head and eyes along with the same movement of your shoulders, the left one moving forward and the right one moving back. Repeat this a few times. You will find that this engagement of the shoulders and upper back enables you to

(continued)

(continued)

see much further to the right. Extend an imaginary line from the tip of your nose to the wall and note where this point has moved to now.

Stop and rest.

Keeping your eyes and your head 'fixed' again, move both shoulders, this time so that the right shoulder moves forward and the left shoulder back. Repeat this several times, paying attention that your head stays motionless and feeling the rotational movement of your upper back. Is it as easy to rotate your shoulders in this direction?

Stop and rest.

Turn your head and eyes now, together with the movement of your right shoulder forward and the left shoulder back. After a few repetitions, stay rotated to the left and extend an imaginary line from the tip of your nose to the wall, noting where this point now is along the horizon.

Stop and rest.

Sit upright again. Place the palms of your hands on your upper legs, near your knees again. Make a small movement of bringing your left knee forward and your right knee a bit back. You will feel a small movement in your pelvis, as if the right sitting bone moves slightly back and your left sitting bone moves slightly forward. Notice that this movement, initiated in your leg and pelvis, moves your head and your eyes slightly to the right.

–   continue moving the left knee forwards and the right one backwards and now let your left shoulder move forwards while your right shoulder moves backwards. You will notice that this movement of your legs, pelvis and now shoulders turns your head and your eyes further to the right. The range of movement around the vertical axis has increased so that you can probably almost see behind you.

Stop and rest.

Now, just move your head and eyes to the right and notice that your legs, pelvis and shoulders will join in, almost automatically.

Place your hands on your legs again. This time, move your right knee slightly forwards while your left knee moves backwards. After repeating this a few times, let your shoulders begin to join in, the right one moving forwards and the left one back. The movement in your legs and pelvis and now shoulders will move your head and neck, so that you can see even further to the left.

- sit and roll back on your sitting bones and bend your entire spine so that your chin comes towards your chest and you are looking downwards and stay there.
- now turn your head to look to the right and to the left, you will experience this limitation. The vertebrae in the chest and neck are designed to rotate when the spine is upright and the head is resting on a vertical axis.

Stop and rest.

The movement of our head and eyes around the vertical axis is important to our survival. In the evolutionary history of human beings, when our predecessors become bi-pedal (able to stand on the back two legs of their four-legged mammalian ancestors), they gained the advantage of having a spine which was now vertical in relation to the legs and to the environment. The ability of the head, the carrier of our sense organs, to rotate on this now vertical axis, enabled them to scan the horizon, noticing prey much more quickly and reacting more effectively to potential threats. This view of the surrounding environment is now being limited by the 'tunnel' vision which may develop from the overuse of concentration focussing on the small area a screen takes up in front of us. When being upright is compromised by postural habits which keep the entire spine slightly flexed and the head looking downwards, so is the ability to perceive the surrounding environment also compromised.

Notes

1 Quoted at the Amherst Training: June 11th 1981.
2 See Health and Safety Executive –Digital screen equipment guidance and regulations. www.hse.gov.uk/msd/dse/
3 Roskos, B (2016). Visual information processing. *The International Encyclopedia of Communication Theory and Philosophy*. 1–12.
4 Pavlidis, GT (1981). Sequencing, eye movements and the early objective diagnosis of dyslexia, in G Pavlidis and T R Miles, *Dyslexia Research and its Application to Education*. Chichester and New York: Wiley and Sons.
5 AS Melrose, RA Graveling, H Cowie, P Ritchie, and RM Mulholland (2007). Better display screen equipment (DSE) work-related ill health data. Institute of Occupational Medicine. Norwich: The Stationery Office.

6 Learning to crawl

Through the first years of life, we organise our entire system in a direction which will forever guide us in that direction. We end up being restricted, we don't do music, we don't do other things. What is most important, we find ourselves capable of doing only those things that we already know.

Moshe Feldenkrais

Case story

'The problem with Derek is that he appears rigid, inflexible, uncoordinated and closed. He looks tense – as if he is about to explode.'

The company is bidding for a major public sector contract worth £300 million over the next five years. Derek has been fundamental in putting the bid together. Over £1 million has been spent preparing the bid documentation. The company has been shortlisted and is required to present their bid before a panel made up of senior civil servants and a junior departmental minister. The bid team is running through the presentation they have been asked to make as part of the bidding process.

Technically for this type of bid marks aren't given for the quality of the presentation – however, from experience, the presentation is often the key for a decision to go the right way. It is an opportunity to show the client what the bidder would be like to work with. At the moment nobody is sure that anyone would want to work with Derek.

Fortunately this is only the run through and there is still enough time for the team to get it right. However, changing presenter is not an option. The client has requested that the key presenter must be the project manager for the contract – and this just happens to be Derek.

Although Derek is a senior manager he generally avoids making presentations. He will normally attend a presentation for a bid he is involved with but only to answer the technical questions posed by the people evaluating the bid. In that role he is extremely comfortable, he is not, however, comfortable presenting and generally avoids having to do so.

'Derek, you are looking particularly tense and uncomfortable, I have to ask, are you feeling ok?'

'No,' he replies, 'I feel awkward, I don't feel in control, I feel clumsy and my back is killing me.'

Introduction

This chapter and the one following explore the path of early physical development that most babies generally proceed through to the point of being able to stand and to walk. This initial learning is important as it allows the central nervous system to develop the neural framework required within the brain that enables a person to move. It is also the point where an individual's self-image – how they perceive themselves within their world – begins to develop.

These early stages of development are precursors for the efficient functioning of an individual. If learning is incomplete, for example through illness, physical or mental disability, or by parents misguidedly trying to speed up the development of the child, there can be a significant impact on the individual's wellbeing throughout the rest of their life. Incomplete or disruption to physical development in early childhood can lead to:

- Poor coordination
- Inability to focus on a task
- Problems with vision and spatial awareness
- Potential difficulties in reading and writing

According to a recent pilot study[1] a large proportion of children in England are starting school without the physical skills that they need to succeed in the classroom. Of the 46 children tested using the Movement Assessment Battery for Children-2[2] when they started school in September 2015, 21 per cent had significant movement difficulties, and a further 8 per cent had movement abilities below what would be expected for their age. In addition to this, the children were tested using the Institute for Neuro-Physiological Psychology (INPP) screening test and between 75 and 90 per cent of the children were displaying signs of neuromotor immaturity[3]. Both of these assessment tools identify symptoms typically associated with ADHD, Aspergers, Dyslexia and Developmental Coordination Disorder (formerly known as dyspraxia). This might suggest that a large proportion of children may not be receiving appropriate movement opportunities in their early years of life (in the home and in the pre-school environment) and that this may potentially impact their behaviour and their learning when they start school. It could well have significant implications on their ability to perform in later life.

In early childhood the learning that takes place through movement becomes 'hardwired' into an individual's brain. If a child successfully navigates the 'stages' of early development then there should be an ease and efficiency of movement. Even so, as a person continues maturing they may develop habits that restrict ease of movement. These habits may initially arise as a response to physical injuries or emotional difficulties, however, after they have fulfilled their initial purpose they could detrimentally affect the quality of life a person experiences.

What constitutes ease of movement will differ from one person to another – it is by its nature a subjective point of view as it relies on personal experience. Many people may not even realise that they have the potential to develop greater ease of movement, taking for granted that the absence of physical pain suggests there is nothing to improve.

And yet the very premise behind Moshe Feldenkrais' research and work challenges this. The absence of pain does not mean that that the human organism is operating as efficiently as it could. As discussed earlier in this book the ability to develop personally depends on the curiosity of the individual. Without it there is no development and choice is limited. The method created by Moshe Feldenkrais partly came about because he was not prepared to accept professional medical opinion that if he was ever going to walk properly again he would need an operation on his seriously damaged knee. He questioned the perceived wisdom of the day. He resolved his problem by using his skills as a scientist and engineer and consequently learnt to walk freely without the need for an operation.

His work with people with cerebral palsy is well documented.[4] At the time medical opinion was that many of these people could not hope to have a functioning life of any quality. Many times he proved that the doctors and specialists were wrong. Using Functional Integration Moshe Feldenkrais would encourage individuals to explore the movements which, on their own, they would not have been capable of undertaking. The movements he facilitated were more often than not those associated with the early stages of maturation. Most of the individuals he worked with discovered possibilities of movement they were incapable of before and in general their overall quality of life increased, in some cases significantly.

Whilst the following question is not necessarily an easy one to answer it is worth asking. What habits of movement have you developed since childhood that may have impinged on your ability to perform as you would like? There may be many – there may be none. However, the exploration of rediscovering the movements of early childhood is both enlightening and fun. It also increases awareness, encourages effective and effortless movement, and, improves self-image and confidence.

Stages of early development

There are many skills the young child must learn to accomplish before being able to crawl and the mastery of these skills is often referred to as a stage of development. Arguably if any of the early developmental stages are not completely mastered there could be an impact on the child's ability to move on to explore more complicated manoeuvres. For example the ability to roll over obviously needs mastering before one can crawl. The list below sets out these stages in the general order that they develop:

- The ability to hold the head upright whilst being carried.
- The ability to roll from side to side while lying on the back.
- The ability to follow hand movements with the eyes, which leads to extension.
- The ability to use the extensors.
- The ability to roll over from the back to lying on the front.
- The ability to sit without support
- The ability to crawl.

The more one observes children as they develop the more fascinating it is to see how each individual seems to follow similar lines of inquiry and exploration. Whilst the term 'stages' are often used to define what may be considered as their achievements, the exploration undertaken by a child is much more nuanced and flexible than the list above suggests. The child will continue to explore different options for movement and locomotion after specific 'achievements' have already been made. For example they will explore numerous variations of rolling over. And if the child masters crawling (and eventually walking) it will not necessarily stop using other ways to move around. It is this playful inquiry that encourages development and learning.

Nevertheless, sometimes the levels of natural inquiry are impeded. For any number of reasons a child may limit (or be prevented from) the exploration of certain movements. Some may even miss out the entire crawling stage.

There is growing concern that recent, and not so recent trends in parenting, may also impinge on the ongoing healthy development of young children. These include:

- Pushchairs and prams with moulded body seats which restrict the exploration of movement that would occur in the older style prams that had flat horizontal surfaces with room to move around.
- A reliance on using screen time to keep young children entertained.
- A lack of time spent playing on the floor.
- The use of baby walkers.
- A desire by parents for children to stand and walk before they are ready.

The benefits of crawling

Crawling is directly associated with:

- The development of fine motor skills of the type required to hold a knife and fork, or a pen.
- Strengthening of the hands, wrists, elbows and shoulders.
- Aiding the development of movement in the ribcage also encouraging effective and healthy breathing.
- The development of contra lateral movement.
- The development of the curvature of the spine essential for future spinal development.
- The development of visual spatial skills and eyesight. Crawling requires the interaction between distances and close seeing essential for three dimensional vision which will also be later used for reading and writing.
- The development of memory, especially memory of location.
- The integration of the right and left hand side of the brain.
- The development of balance.
- The development of self autonomy and decision making.
- The development of social emotional skills and the development of confidence.

The opinion of many experts[5] specialising within the field of early years is that the development of physical movement, and in particular crawling, is essential for the successful maturation of the entire nervous system.

Lack of development, as commented on earlier, can detrimentally affect balance, coordination, eye sight, memory, attention, breathing, speech, reading and writing.

In the Feldenkrais Method a great deal of attention is paid to the movements associated with early stages of childhood development. In Awareness Through Movement classes and one-to-one lessons in Functional Integration these movements can be explored, re-learnt or even learnt for the first time. People who regularly undertake classes and lessons will frequently comment personally on the perceived benefits of doing so, citing improvements in co-ordination, balance, visual awareness, breathing, speech and general ease of movement. However, empirical research to validate these experiences is difficult particularly as the researchers have to contend with many variables. Nevertheless, advancements made since the 1990's in neurological research and certainly those following on from the development of Functional Magnetic Resonance Imaging (fMRI) means we are beginning to understand much more clearly how the brain functions and why the Feldenkrais Method could well achieve the results that its advocates claim.[6]

Of particular interest in the field of neuroscience is the development of the theory of neuroplasticity. Neuroplasticity is a term used to describe the brain's ability, if given the right environment, to acquire more efficient patterns of movement and/or rediscover lost or damaged functions of movement. The brain is able to adapt its organisation, structure and function throughout the whole of a person's lifetime. In other words it is possible to re-programme the brain. Other parts of the brain can take over functions that have been lost through damage to other areas. It also enables new patterns of movement to be developed. This is exactly what Moshe Feldenkrais came to understand through his research. He successfully applied his theories to the development of his method and the results can clearly be seen in the available videos of his work.[7] Moshe Feldenkrais has sometimes been described as an early neuroplastician and certainly his early theories of how the brain works have been largely validated.

Returning to his premise that any action always involves thinking, feeling (emotion), sensation, and movement it is possible to see that, according to the principles of neuroplasticity, the learning and refining of movement (such as crawling) through Awareness Through Movement lessons could have a significant and beneficial impact on personal performance, health and well being.

Learning to crawl: Derek's experience

In addition to the work with his coach it was suggested that Derek should go and see a Feldenkrais practitioner. He went and had several lessons in

Functional Integration and started to attend regular Awareness Through Movement classes. He discovered through conversations with his mother, that as a baby he had skipped the crawling stage and spent most of the time shuffling around (quite effectively and quickly) on his bottom before eventually learning to walk. At the age of three he slipped on a tiled floor. This resulted in a spiral fracture of right fibula (one of the two bones in the lower leg). Throughout his life he had always had difficulty with balance and coordination. He couldn't ride a bike until he was fourteen and confessed that he was frequently confused between his left and right hand side.

After several months he observed a very noticeable difference in his sense of balance commenting that in the past he would not have been able to carry a tray with tea cups down the stairs from the bedroom – now he was able to. His confidence improved as did his personal levels of impact and presence. Possibly the benefits came too late as the company lost the bid to a competitor. Nevertheless Derek continues to work for the company and has recently been promoted.

Awareness Through Movement lesson: re-experiencing learning to crawl

For an adult, it is an eye-opening experience to re-visit the learning which took place during the first year of life. As a baby, you learned more in that one year than you will ever learn in any other one year of the rest of your life. We can look back now and have tremendous respect for the intelligence, problem-solving abilities and perseverance of the young baby.

For this lesson, you will need to lie on a slightly cushioned surface which is firm but doesn't create so much friction that you have difficulty making sliding movements – you will need to start at the already advanced stage of being able to lie on your front.

Many people are not comfortable at first in this position. It is not as simple as lying on your back. The dilemmas that first occur are: how to organise my legs? My arms? And what to do with my head? So, let's look at them, one by one.

You will find that most likely you spontaneously placed the heels of both feet either towards one another, with the toes outwards, or you placed the heels outwards, with your toes near to one another. For now, just be sure that your kneecaps (which are more boney than they were in your first year of life) are comfortable in the position you have chosen. As the movements in the lesson progress, you will find the position of your feet which is most comfortable for both lying as well as for moving your legs.

The position of your arms will change during the lesson and to start with, you will want to bend both arms at the elbows and position your upper arms as an extension of your shoulders (at an approximate 90 degree angle to the sides of your torso). Let your lower arms rest on the floor, so that they are approximately parallel to the sides of your torso, with the palms of your hands on the floor.

The position of your head is more challenging. If you turn your head in one direction so that the side of your face rests on the floor, you may feel that this is not so comfortable in your neck. Try the other direction and choose the one which is most comfortable. Notice what part of the side of your face is in contact with the floor, as this will alter with the steps of the lesson. If at any point, the position of leaving your head turned becomes too uncomfortable, take a rest and bring your head to the middle – you can bring your hands on top of one another and use them up as a 'cushion' on which to rest your forehead. You can do this as often as needed, then return to the movements.

The instructions are going to be worded as if you have your head turned to the right, with the left side of your face resting on the floor. If you are more comfortable with your head turned to the left, then change 'right' and 'left' in the instructions.

Bring your right arm so that the palm of your hand can be on the floor and your elbow above your wrist (in the air), so that you could push away from the floor:

– press with your right palm and feel that this movement travels through your lower arm, elbow, upper arm and begins to lift your right shoulder; feel how your shoulder blade slides towards your spine, then stop pressing and let your shoulder return to where it was at the start. Repeat this movement a number of times, stopping at the point where your shoulder blade doesn't slide any further. Feel how your head rolls somewhat and the contact you make with the side of your face and the floor moves more towards your left ear.

Stop and rest. In the rest, you will want to let your forearm come back down to the floor and you may change anything in the organisation of your head and arms, then return to the starting position.

(continued)

(continued)

With your right arm again in the position with the palm of your hand on the floor and your elbow above your wrist:

–   press with your right palm again, moving the shoulder blade towards your spine and when you can go no further, begin to lift your head slightly. Lifting your head and keeping your head, neck and upper back moving together as one unit, you will find your chest in the front will also come slightly away from the floor. You need the support of your hand, your arm and your upper back for the weight of your head to be lifted away from the floor, without much effort. Let your head and shoulder return to the floor, then repeat this movement gently. When your head is lifted, begin to look with your eyes, over your right shoulder; you will feel a slight rotational movement in much of your spine.

Stop and rest in a restful position.

This may seem like a small and simple movement to do as an adult, although I imagine some of you will struggle to find it easy. Imagine if your head was one fifth of your body weight (your head now is about one tenth of your entire weight), as it was when you were first discovering this movement, you will understand how you need the power of your arms and your upper back in order to lift such a heavy weight. Your neck muscles are not strong enough to do this on their own. This is a major accomplishment for a baby. At this stage of development, the baby can now begin to balance and control the movements of its head and can now lie on its front without its head being too heavy to move.

Turn your head to look to the left and have the right side of your face resting on the floor. Bring your left palm to rest on the floor, so that your elbow is supported in the air above your wrist and begin to press now with your left palm so that this pressure moves through your lower arm, elbow and upper arm to slide your left shoulder blade in the direction of your spine. Repeat this movement slowly and carefully, as turning in this direction may not be as easy as in the direction you first chose.

Stop and rest.

Return to the starting position: head turned to the left, left palm on the floor, elbow above the wrist. Press with your hand again and once your shoulder blade slides as far as it can in the direction of your spine, lift your head, together with your upper spine and after a few repetitions, begin to look over your left shoulder.

Stop and rest.

Place both palms on the floor, with elbows above your wrists; begin with your head turned to the right:

– press with your right hand, feel the transmission of the movement, slide your shoulder blade and lift your head to look over your right shoulder; now move your head to look straight ahead, as if you are looking towards the horizon. At this point, your left shoulder would have lifted so that both shoulders are on the same level. Press with your left hand to bring the left shoulder higher and let the right shoulder drop down towards the floor and allow your head to turn to look to the left, then over the left shoulder. Let your head come down and rest on the floor.
– Repeat this movement, beginning with the left hand pressing, lift your head, turn it to look straight ahead, then turn it to the right and let it return to the floor.
– Repeat these movements, going right and left – you have now learned to lift your head, to be able to see the horizon and to turn to the other side.

Stop and rest. Turn over to rest on your back for a while. Roll your head slowly to the right and to the left, feeling how the rolling movement involves much of your upper spine.

Learning to lift the head, to see the horizon and to be able to turn it from side to side is another big step in a baby's development. Up until this point, the baby has spent most of its life lying on its back and in turning its head right and left, and its view of the surrounding environment was limited. In the position of lying on the front, lifting the head and being able to look over and behind each shoulder, the baby gains nearly a 360 degree view of its environment.

Lie on your front again, turn your head in the direction which is easier for you. The instructions will be given as if you have turned your head to the right. Bring your right arm to the position with your palm

(continued)

(continued)

on the floor, your elbow above your wrist, but this time, let your left arm lie alongside your torso, with the back of your hand on the floor:

–   press with your right hand to lift your shoulder and leaving your head on the floor this time, begin to slide it downwards, moving your face into the space created by your hand and your lifted right shoulder so that you can look downwards towards your pelvis, then slide your head back to the starting position. You may start to feel a small movement of the right side of your pelvis lifting slightly away from the floor; keep this movement to a minimum at this stage of the lesson. Repeat this movement gently and slowly a number of times.

Stop and rest.

Return to the same starting position; this time leave your right arm bent, but with the elbow resting on the floor; the left arm is still lying alongside your torso:

–   lift the right side of your pelvis slightly, feeling the weight roll onto the left side; you will feel a small amount of rotation in your lower back and more rotation in your lower ribs, as the right side will lift slightly away from the floor and the left side will press slightly into the floor.

This movement will begin to feel limited by the position of your right knee. You can now make this easier by rotating your leg so that the right kneecap is facing outwards, enabling the inside of your lower right leg to be in contact with the floor. Repeat this movement of lifting the right side of the pelvis, and at the point where it doesn't move any further easily, rotate the leg so that the knee turns outwards and now begin to slightly bend your right knee, letting your right lower leg slide on the floor, returning to the starting position each time.

Stop and rest.

With your right arm bent, your right elbow in the air and above your wrist, press with your hand to lift your right shoulder and as you begin to slide your head downwards, simultaneously, lift the right side of your pelvis, let your right knee bend and slide your right knee upwards while your head is sliding downwards. Your knee and your face will slowly approach one another and you will feel your right side bending. Repeat this movement a number of times, each time returning both your head and leg to the starting position.

Stay at a place where your face and your knee are a comfortable distance from one another and lower your right elbow now to rest on the floor. You will find that it is much more comfortable to have your head turned to the right when your pelvis is also turned and your knee is bent. This is a position in which many babies at this stage of development will sleep and some of you may recognise this position as one in which you are comfortable sleeping. And it is very similar to the 'recovery' position in first aid.

Start again, but with your head turned to the left; your right arm is now lying alongside your torso and your left palm is on the floor with your elbow in the air above your wrist:

- press with your left hand so that your left shoulder lifts and you can begin to slide your head into the space created by your left hand and your lifted shoulder, looking downwards towards your pelvis. You may feel that you 'automatically' lift the left side of your pelvis at the same time, as you have learned that this makes it easier in your experience on the first side. In order to feel the full potential of rotation in the upper part of your back, minimise the lifting of your pelvis at this point in the sequence. Repeat this movement a few times.

Stop and rest.

With your head turned to the left again, and your right arm lengthened alongside your torso and your left arm bent, this time with your elbow on the floor:

- begin to lift the left side of your pelvis, feeling the weight shift onto the right side. Rotate your left leg so that your kneecap can face outwards, enabling you to gradually begin to bend your left knee so that your pelvis can rotate further and you can feel the rotation moving upwards along your back.

(continued)

(continued)

Stop and rest.

Now place your left palm on the floor with your elbow in the air and above your left wrist: as you press with your hand and lift your shoulder and begin to direct your face to move underneath your arm, simultaneously rotate your pelvis so that your left knee can bend and you can slide your left knee towards your face and your face more towards your knee, feeling your entire left side bending.

Stay where your knee and your head are a comfortable distance from one another and lower your left arm to the floor and rest in this position.

Place both arms on either side of your head with the palms on the floor, elbows above the wrists:

– turn your head to the right, press with the right hand to lift your shoulder, slide your head downwards while your pelvis rolls to enable your right knee to bend, bring your face and knee towards one another. As you return, lift your head so that you can turn it to the left (you learned how to do this at the beginning of this lesson) and now move your head, keeping it slightly lifted, roll your pelvis and bend your knee, bringing your face and left knee closer. You can now do this on one side, then the other. This is the beginning of crawling.

Slowly find your way to standing; begin to walk around and notice how these simple movements have affected your walking.

Notes

1 Duncombe, R and Preedy, P (2016) *Movement for Learning?* Paper presented at Building Brighter Futures – Let's Start Together, Leicester, UK (September).

2 Henderson, S E, Sugden, D A and Barnett, A L (2007) *Movement assessment battery for children–2*. London: Pearson.

3 Goddard Blythe, S A (2012). *Assessing neuromotor readiness for learning. The INPP developmental screening test and school intervention programme.* Chichester: Wiley-Blackwell.

4 For example see Norman Doidge. *The Brain's Way of Healing.* New York: Penguin Books.

5 For example see the Institute for Neuro-Physiological Psychology.

6 Clark D, Schumann F and Mostofsky S H (2015) Mindful movement and skilled attention. *Frontiers of Human Neuroscience.* 9:297.

7 The International Feldenkrais Federation have videos of Moshe Feldenkrais working with individuals with cerebral palsy. See www.feldenkrais-method.org

7   Learning to walk

the proper posture of the body is such that it can initiate movement in any direction with the same ease; that it can start any movement without a preliminary adjustment; that the movement is performed with the minimum of work.[1]

Moshe Feldenkrais

Case story

Phillip is sitting in a cafe having a coffee.

'Why is it that Simon[2] walks so gracefully? He never used to.'

'Well, how do you walk? What do you sense about yourself as you walk?'

'I've never really ever thought about it before – I just place one foot in front of the other.'

'Well ok – look around and observe how people are walking. What do you see? What messages are they sending out in the way they walk? What is your sense about who they are?'

Phillip looks around at the various people entering the cafe. These are a mixture of people from all walks of life; however, the majority are business executives like Phillip. A group of young executives come through the door following a person who appears to be their line manager.

'Well they are all quite different. Did you notice that last group though? They all walked in a similar way. Overall they seemed stiff and inflexible with very little movement in their lower body. The way

(continued)

(continued)

they were swinging their arms you would have thought they were lifting weights. To be honest they looked as if they were trying to look strong and confident. In my opinion they looked frightened.'
    'Well how do you walk?'
    'Well not like that I hope. I don't do I?'

Introduction

Whilst there are other primates who can walk on two legs (as well as four), human beings are unique in as much they are solely bipedal. At some point in evolutionary history Homo sapiens progressed towards efficiency of movement at the cost of strength and speed. Survival of the fittest depends on a species' ability to find food. The Homo sapiens answer to this dilemma was to walk on two legs. Walking in this way uses less calories enabling the remaining calories to be used for other purposes. For Homo sapiens this resulted in the ongoing development of a complex brain that would eventually require 16 times more energy than muscles do to operate optimally. On a daily basis, 25 per cent of our calorific energy is diverted to the brain. Whilst this early development cost our species speed and strength it promoted resilience in movement and the development of a brain capable of the abstract thinking required for complex planning.

The human body is capable of greater endurance than many other animals, being able to move over much greater distances on a daily basis. The efficiency of movement and the endurance it produced was particularly important in the early hunter-gatherer societies. Whilst the hunters could not run at the same speed as the animals they were chasing, they could follow them for such periods of time that the hunted animal would collapse from exhaustion.

One of the other benefits of being able to walk on two legs was that it freed the hands to do other things such as holding tools.

In most cultures learning to walk is considered an important achievement and a major landmark in the development of a child. This is possibly because out of all the forms of locomotion it is the one which most represents the development of independence and maturity. The child no longer relies on others to move from one place to another. As soon as there is locomotion, a child is more freely able to explore and discover. Sometimes the cultural importance placed on walking can lead parents to worry unnecessarily about when their child will begin to walk.

There is, of course, no optimum age by which a healthy child should be able to walk and each child will differ, depending on upbringing and circumstance. Even after the child has taken its first steps she/he will continue to learn, refining the movement over many years. After the first few faltering steps have been taken, a child quite often finds it easier to continue her/his exploration of the world through the other forms of locomotion she/he has already learnt. This is quite natural as in the child's early stages of development their legs grow increasingly in mass more than they do in strength.

Stages of development

In the previous chapter the skills that a child needs to accomplish before they could crawl were listed. As mentioned the acquisition of these skills is often defined as specific stages of development and most children, except those born with a disability, will be observed to follow similar lines of inquiry.

The following are the developmental stages that can generally be observed as the child learns to walk.

- Through crawling the child continues to develop the physical strength required for upward movement.
- The movement of both legs and feet become more refined and controlled.
- The child is able to stand from a sitting position and learns to squat.
- The child starts to cruise, i.e. the ability to move around in a standing position using furniture of appropriate height for support.
- Starts to walk.

What constitutes an adequate attainment of any stage has been the subject of much research, a fair amount of which can appear to be inconclusive because of the difficulty in getting young infants to undertake activities that can be empirically measured. How many forms of crawling should a person be able to achieve before the skill is so well mastered that they develop in a more functionally integrated way? Some children appear to miss out the crawling stage completely and move straight to walking. Is this important?

As we discussed in the last chapter many specialists in early child learning consider that all the 'developmental stages' need to be mastered to prevent arrested development becoming a problem in later life.[3] In developing his method Moshe Feldenkrais researched the early stages of development in babies and children and discovered aspects of organic learning which he concluded were fundamental to any later experience of learning.

From his perspective the key to personal development is flexibility and having choice. Much of the potential for this choice derives from our organic learning as children as we try out a varying number of approximations to achieve locomotion. The human species operates in an environment that is dynamic and constantly changing. If you only have a limited number of movement strategies to select from you are disadvantaged. It is our ability to improvise and modify the variety of movements we have in our repertoire that enables us to cope (or not) with the changing landscape we live in.

Efficiency in movement

The way in which each person walks, often referred to as the gait, differs to such an extent that many people are able to recognise one another from a distance by simply observing the way in which they walk. Some of these differences will be the result of body structure, size and weight, and early development as discussed above. Other differences will result from past injuries, fashion (in particular what a person choses to wear on their feet), and social mores (for example the idea that men shouldn't swing their hips when they walk). Some people appear to move in a ponderous heavy fashion whilst others seem to levitate. The walk of a confident, successful individual is often extremely different from a person who is depressed and unhappy.

Walking requires the integration of the whole body – it is a somatic process. Locomotion starts with an intention to move to somewhere in order to do something. This intention is transferred into messages that are instantaneously issued to all parts of the body preparing it to move. The whole process of walking is sometimes referred to as 'controlled falling'. It requires all parts of the muscular skeletal system to work together in order to maintain balance and direction.

The walking cycle is comprised of three stages. If the person is in standing with both feet together, a decision is made to lift one leg forward. In order to do this the 'supporting' leg, (i.e. the one which is not being lifted from the ground and therefore is supporting the weight of the person), will move from 'standing' stage, (where the contact and pressure of the foot is predominantly through the heel to the ground), to a 'mid-standing' stage. This is where the pressure of the foot starts transferring from the heel towards the ball of the foot. Finally the foot moves into the 'propulsion' stage where the toes bend and the force generated is used to lift the foot and leg off the floor in a forward direction.

At the same time the weight of the body will be transferred to the forward foot which will now becomes the 'supporting' foot as it makes contact to the floor through the heel. At this point the knee will bend slightly so the shock of the contact can be transmitted through the rest of the skeleton.

As the leg and foot continue its movement beyond the 'supporting' foot, the knee of the 'supporting' foot straightens out and lifts the body and the cycle continues.

Ease of movement depends on the mobility of the pelvis. As Moshe Feldenkrais explained 'All correct action starts with the movement of the pelvis which displaces itself so as to carry the spine and the head through to the new position while allowing the head complete freedom of movement. The control of the head and of the pelvis are, therefore, absolutely essential to all correct action. One is not more important than the other. Both must be controlled correctly to obtain correct action. In some acts the position of the head is more telling and easier to notice, but it cannot be obtained without proper control of the pelvis.'[4]

Inefficiency in movement

If you watch people out and about you can see through the variety of ways they move that many are not walking in a way that is efficient. How the muscular skeletal system is organised is fundamentally important for efficient walking and yet, as indicated previously, this organisation is often inhibited by fashion, and social mores.

The shoes that people often wear are generally not helpful towards efficiency in movement. The problem is that most shoes are not shaped like healthy feet. The toes are often squeezed together and modern fashion, especially for women, encourages high heels. The way the foot operates, and especially the toes, is vital for effective locomotion. The feet are the reference point in their contact with the ground. The toes are sensitive and through their contact with the ground pick up a great deal of information about the terrain. This information is transferred through the central nervous system making adjustments throughout the whole of the muscular skeletal system enabling us to remain upright. The toes should naturally splay when placed on the ground. Through the wearing of shoes this sensitivity is reduced and it can affect balance. If you place your feet on the ground you should see a small space between each toe. If you can't then your feet may not be functioning as well as they could.

The problem with any form of cushioning of the heel is that it changes the impact with the ground together with the way the body copes with the relationship with gravity. As indicated above the heel along with the knee acts as a shock absorber. It deals with the 'ground reaction force' that occurs when we place the foot on the ground. Generally on hard surfaces whatever pressure is placed on the ground an equal amount of force is pushed back in nearly the opposite direction. The ground reaction force helps an individual to stay upright. However, certain styles of shoes prevent this occurring, especially shoes with high heels. The loss of contact with the ground may result in problems with feet, ankles, knees, and hip joints, in later life.

One of the other key factors leading to inefficiencies in walking is the rather bizarre belief that individuals, particularly men, should not move their pelvis as it is not masculine. This often leads to the type of walking described in the above case story. The reality is that for efficient and physically healthy movement the pelvis needs to rotate.

If a person walks in a way that can result in deformed feet, rigidity of the pelvis, a lack of rotational movement in the spine, restriction in the fluidity of movement in the rib cage, lack of flexibility in the sternum, rigidity in the shoulder girdle, and a lack of flexibility in the movement of the arms, then that individual can expect a certain degree of physical difficulty.

Walking as communication

The manner in which a person walks is a form of non-verbal communication that everyone can read. All sorts of conclusions will be drawn, possibly incorrectly, about a person from their gait. This is an emotional reaction that is natural. It is an evolutionary defence mechanism under the control of the limbic system. It enables individuals to perceive danger by making evaluations about another's personality and intentions. However, this leaves us with several questions that we could ask ourselves.

- How do I walk?
- Do I walk in a way that is efficient?
- Do I walk in a way that portrays confidence, ease and health?
- Do I walk in a way that communicates what I wish to communicate?

Awareness Through Movement lesson: learning to walk

Learning to crawl, which you would have experienced in the Awareness Through Movement lesson with Chapter 6, begins to develop the skills which will next lead to crawling on all fours and the transition to standing and walking.

First, let's go further back in the baby's development and experience the foundation for learning to walk which began, time-wise, quite a way previous to any intention of standing or walking.

Lie on your back (your legs are straight and your arms lying at your sides) on a comfortable surface. Feel how you make contact with the floor: where do you feel more contact, where is there less contact, do you feel more contact overall on your right side than on your left side?

Bend each leg, one at a time, so that your foot is flat on the floor and your knees are 'balanced' above your ankles and your feet are a comfortable distance apart.

This starting position may not be as easy to find as you would imagine. If you experiment a bit, first with the distance between your feet, you will find that as you move your feet closer together (so that they touch), your knees will tend to fall outwards and you need to hold on with the muscles on the inside of your legs. If you now move your feet so that they are far apart, your knees will tend to fall inwards and you will have to engage the muscles on the outside of your legs. If you find a distance between your feet where your knees can 'rest' above your ankles, you will not need to engage either the muscles on the inside, or on the outside of your legs. This is a mechanically efficient position which requires little energy to stay there.

There is another factor and that is the distance of your feet from your pelvis. Once you have found the comfortable distance between your feet, slide your feet so that your heels move away from your buttocks and you will begin to 'unbend' your knees. You will feel the muscles in the front of your thighs begin to contract in order to stop your legs from 'slipping'. If you slide your heels closer to your buttocks, you may reach a place where you begin to feel a strain in your knees. You want to find a position for your feet and thereby your legs which is balanced and requires the least amount of muscular effort just to keep your legs standing.

Interlace your fingers and place your hands behind your head so that the part of the back of your head which was making contact with the floor is now lying in the palms of your hands:

- bring your elbows slightly towards one another, then lift your head slightly away from the floor. As you lift your head, let your chin move towards your chest and your eyes look to the space in between your legs. You will feel that the front of your neck gets shorter and, at the same time, the back of your neck will get a bit longer.
- as you repeat this movement gently, you will feel gradually that your shoulders lift slightly from the floor, your breastbone (sternum) sinks downwards slightly. You will find this movement easier if you breathe out with the movement of lifting your head.

(continued)

(continued)

Stop and rest, let your legs lengthen and your arms rest at your sides. Notice if any part of your upper back, or shoulders lie differently from how they were lying at the start.

Bend your legs again; interlace your fingers, put them behind your head, bring your elbows towards one another and lift your head again

– now begin to lift your right foot from the floor, bending at the hip joint to bring your right knee in the direction of your right elbow, while your right elbow moves in the direction of your right knee. You will feel the right side of your back lengthen and the lower ribs press slightly into the floor. Repeat this a number of times, comfortably and without any ambition to bring the knee and the elbow any closer.

Stop and rest, let your legs lengthen and your arms rest at yours sides. Notice if the right side of your back is resting with any more contact than the left side.

This movement may be familiar to you, if you know it as a part of an exercise. It is often used to increase flexibility by making great efforts to bring the knee and the elbow closer together. As an 'exercise,' this movement engages certain abdominal muscles which may be 'strengthened' by many repetitions.

But we are using this movement very differently. By doing it slowly and using only a comfortable amount of effort and by not using any force to attempt to shorten the distance between the elbow and the knee, the flexor muscles in the front of the torso are being engaged while the extensor muscles in your back are being quietly lengthened.

When a muscle is engaged, the muscle fibres contract, thereby shortening the distance between the origin and the insertion of the muscle. The attachments of muscles are usually to bones, which are then brought closer together when a muscle contracts. When a muscle is not contracting, its fibres can rest and the muscle can be 'lengthened' as the bones move apart.

When you come to rest after bringing your right elbow and right knee towards one another, you may feel that the right side of your back feels longer and rests with more contact to the floor. If so, this is because the flexor muscles in the front of your chest have been contracting, allowing the extensor muscles of your back to come to their resting length. These muscles are often habitually in contraction and they don't get much opportunity to rest.

Bend your legs, interlace your fingers, put your hands behind your head, lift your head again and this time, begin to lift your left foot from the floor, bringing your left knee in the direction of your left elbow. Keep repeating this movement, bringing your chin towards your chest, letting your breastbone sink and breathing out slowly, lifting your leg simultaneously, then return to the floor each time. This movement may feel very different on the left side from what it felt like on the right side.

Stop and rest, let your legs lengthen and your arms rest at your sides. Feel if your left side is now contacting the floor differently and if it is more like your right side.

Bend your legs, interlace your fingers, put your hands behind your head, bring your elbows towards one another, lift your head again and this time rotate your head, arms and upper back slightly to the left, as if you want to bring your right elbow slightly over to the left. After repeating this a few times, lift your left leg so that you can bring your left knee in the direction of your right elbow while, at the same time, bringing your right elbow in the direction of your left knee. Repeat a number of times, returning your head and your foot to the floor each time.

Stop and rest, letting your legs lengthen and your arms lie at your sides.

In your imagination, draw a line from your right shoulder joint down to your left hip joint and sense how it travels diagonally across the front of your chest. Now in your imagination draw a line from your left shoulder joint to your right hip. You will probably find that the first line is more clear and easier to imagine.

The first movement in this lesson, of bringing your right elbow and your right knee towards one another, is a 'uni-lateral' movement, taking place on the same side. The above movement of bringing your right elbow and your left knee towards one another is a 'cross-lateral' movement. It is an important stage in a baby's development when it makes a connection between the right and left sides. We will soon see how this is one of the foundation movements for walking.

(continued)

(continued)

Bend your legs, interlace your fingers, put your hands behind your head, bring your elbows towards one another, lift your head and rotate your head, arms and upper back to the right, as if you want to bring your left elbow over to the right. If you are right-handed, this direction will seem less familiar than rotating in the first direction. After a few repetitions, begin to lift your right leg so that you can bring your left elbow towards your right knee, while bringing your right knee towards your left elbow. Repeat this a number of times, until you begin to feel that this diagonal movement has become familiar.

Stop and rest, letting your legs lengthen and your arms rest at your sides. In your imagination, draw a line from your left shoulder to your right hip joint and notice if this imaginary line is now clearer.

Slowly, roll to one side, come to sit, then find a way to come to stand. Walk around and notice if your walking feels different. Perhaps you can feel a connection between your right arm and your left leg, which travels through your torso when stepping onto your left foot and a connection between your left arm and right leg, when stepping onto your right foot. You have now discovered the all-important cross-lateral relationship which is so crucial to coordinated and easy walking.

Come back down to the floor, but this time on your hands and knees – let's call this position 'on all fours.' You may need some extra padding under your knees, as they are not as soft as they were when you first mastered this position as a baby. Check that your hip-joints are above your knees and your shoulder joints are above your wrists and that you have equal amounts of weight on your knees and on your hands.

– lift your right hand from the floor and place it back on the floor, just forward of where you were, as if taking a 'step' with your arm. Let some weight shift into your hand, then lift it and bring it back to the starting position. Feel how your weight shifts over to your left side, to allow you to 'unweight' your right side, then returns to equal distribution.

Come off your hands and your knees and sit to rest.

Return to the 'all fours' position:

– lift your right leg and bring it forward, again, as if 'taking a step' with your leg. Feel how your weight shifts over to your left leg to

'unweight' your right leg, making it easier to move it forward. Let the weight shift onto your right knee slowly so that there is time to 'absorb' the weight, rather than 'bang' your knee on the floor.
- slide your right knee forward as far as you can easily and find out how you can slowly let the right buttock come down to the floor, so that you are now sitting in a side saddle like position.

Rest in this position and feel how easy it can be to return to 'all fours' from this side saddle sitting. Now that you are back on 'all fours':

- simultaneously lift both your right hand and right knee and take a step forward with both, then return. In order to do this, you will feel how much your weight will shift onto the left side.

Slide your right leg far forward again so that you can slowly lower your right buttock to the floor and rest in side-saddle sitting.

Come back to the 'all fours' position:

- this time lift your left hand and take a step forward, letting the weight shift onto your arm, then return. Repeat this a number of times.

Stop and rest.

Return to 'all fours':

- take a step with your left leg only; then let your hand join in, so that you can now take a step forward, then return.
- slide your left leg forward as far as you can and slowly let your left buttock come to the floor so that you can sit in side saddle in the opposite configuration. You will find that sitting in this side saddle position will feel different, according to which leg is bent behind.

Rest in this side saddle position.

Return to 'all fours':

- lift both your right hand and right leg and take a step forward, then lift both your left hand and left leg and take a step forward. You have now accomplished unilateral crawling – the second

(continued)

(continued)

stage in mastering crawling. You may find that you have to shift quite far onto the opposite hand and leg in order to propel yourself forwards. Using this form of locomotion, you will soon find that you cannot move very fast.

Rest, then return to 'all fours':

– this time bring your right leg and left hand forward simultaneously, alternating with bringing your left leg and right hand forward; this is the cross-lateral and final stage of crawling. You will find that you can keep your torso more in the centre, allowing for faster movement of your limbs.

Rest in sitting, then make a transition to standing.

– take a step forward with your right foot, while bringing your right arm forward at the same time; follow this with a step forward, bringing your left foot and left arm forward at the same time. You will feel how awkward this pattern of walking is, though you will observe some people who use it.
– now take a step forward with your right foot, letting your left arm move forward simultaneously; follow this with a step forward with your left foot while your right arm swings forward. This is the more familiar cross-lateral walk, which allows us to remain balanced in the upright position.

As this lesson in Awareness Through Movement takes you through many months of organic learning in a small amount of time, I am sure it enables you to appreciate the amount of time it takes a baby to develop the many skills needed to finally be able to stand and walk.

Notes

1 Moshe Feldenkrais (1999), Body and mature behavior: a study of anxiety, sex, gravitation, and learning. London: Routledge.
2 Simon was introduced in Chapter 3.
3 For example see the Institute for Neuro-physiological Psychology.
4 Moshe Feldenkrais (1990). *Awareness through movement: easy to do health exercises to improve your posture, vision, imagination, and personal awareness.* New York: HarperCollins.

8   Learning to talk

The more an individual advances his development the greater will be his ease of action.[1]

Moshe Feldenkrais

Case story

Jenny is a business development manager for a large international charity. The charity's UK training director has suggested she has some executive coaching with an emphasis on her communication skills and the way in which she uses her voice.

Jenny is particularly curious and eager to learn anything that will help develop her career. She is relatively small in height (5' 2") and equally slim. In the first session she explains that she believes that the sound of her voice is related to her small stature. The pitch of her voice is high and the overall tone has little harmonic resonance, (people had described it as sounding 'thin and reedy'). She explains that she finds it difficult to control her voice when she is nervous or excited. In such situations the voice moves to a higher register and she starts to speak at an increasingly fast pace.

As she explains this she fidgets with a ring on her finger, plays with her watch strap, scratches her leg, and picks at her ear. At the same time she is lifting her right heel up and down off the floor. When this is pointed out to her she replies that she was not aware of what she had been doing.

Introduction

When the movement of others is considered there can be a tendency to regard it as something that is observed, and of course it is. However, the state of an individual can also be heard through the sound of their voice. Speaking is an action and therefore consists of thought, feeling, sensation and movement. Whilst certain specific parts of the body are used to create the physical sound of the voice, the whole organisation of the muscular skeletal system will affect tonal quality.

Many people are sensitive about the sound of their voice. It is something uniquely personal to everyone. Feedback concerning how we use our voice can be difficult to receive. One of the issues is that many people believe they cannot do anything to change the sound of their voice, even if they actually wanted to do so. Significant conclusions are often made about a person based on the sound of their voice alone, this includes assumptions concerning another's intelligence and motivation. Some people are deemed to have beautiful voices; others are not.

The voice is an essential tool for communicating thoughts and ideas with the world around us. Many of us depend on a well functioning voice in order to make a living. Yet it is probably the one part of the body that people know the least about.

The basic components

Sound is generated from the vibration of what are called the 'true' vocal folds. These folds are fibro-elastic ligaments covered by a mucous membrane. In a mature woman they are approximately 17mm long and in men approximately 23mm. The vocal folds are attached to the thyroid and cricoid cartilage at the front of the neck (more commonly known as the Adam's apple) and two moveable cartilages at the back called the arytenoids. The whole structure (which also includes the epiglottis and hyoid bone) is referred to as the larynx (vocal box) and is situated within the vocal tract. The vocal tract lies above the trachea with the larynx at its base. The vocal folds are also attached to the surrounding wall of the larynx by the laryngeal musculature.

When we breathe the arytenoids move apart, opening the vocal folds like a pair of curtains. When we decide to speak or sing they move together closing the vocal folds. Sound is generated when the air pressure from the lungs pushes against the closed vocal folds causing them to open and shut very quickly, creating an audible vibration of sound. It is a similar process to how sound can be made by stretching the mouthpiece of a fully blown balloon and allowing the air to escape slowly.

The pitch of your voice; whether it sounds high or low, is determined by the length and tension of the vocal folds controlled very precisely by the laryngeal musculature, the overall position of the Adam's apple within the vocal tract and it's relationship to the arytenoids. Place a finger gently on your Adam's apple and sing a sound like a siren. Start by singing a low note and raising the pitch to as high as you can comfortably. As the pitch gets higher you should notice that your Adam's apple moves upwards (it is in fact lengthening the vocal folds away from the arytenoids). Generally, as the Adam's apple moves upwards there is more tension in the vocal folds and the pitch is higher. Imagine plucking an elastic band. The greater the tension in the elastic band, the higher the sound. If you reduce the tension the sound becomes lower.

Although the sound is formed within the vocal tract, words are formed in your mouth, with the exception of 'm', 'n' and 'ing' which are formed in the nasal cavity. Articulation depends primarily on the use of your tongue, lips and jaw.

The quality of the sound (timbre) that a person produces when they speak or sing is often referred to as the resonance of the voice. There are two types of vocal resonance; resonant amplification, and resonant vibration.

Resonant amplification relates to the amount of vibration generated by your voice within certain cavities in the body, generally the pharynx, the mouth, the chest, sinuses and the nose. The quality of sound is determined by the position of the Adam's apple and the amount of air pressure generated from the lungs. When it is positioned high within the larynx the vocal tract becomes short and narrow and the sound will predominantly vibrate within the pharynx, mouth, sinuses and nose, resulting in what is sometimes called the 'head' voice. When the position of the Adam's apple is lower, the vocal tract becomes long and wide allowing more space for amplification to occur, resulting in what is sometimes referred to as the 'chest' voice.

Resonant vibration occurs when an object is made to vibrate at the same rate as the sound source hitting it. Any part of your body (tissue, organs and bones) will resonate in this way to the vibration of your voice, changing the overall quality of its sound.

However, as previously mentioned, the way in which your muscular skeletal system is organised will impact in the way your voice resonates. So, for example, the quality of sound you create will be different if you are slumped over a desk than it would if you were sitting upright. This is because your posture dictates the areas and space in which the sound of the voice can resonate.

The voice has two distinct registers often referred to as 'modal' and 'falsetto'. When we speak it is the modal register we will generally use, not the falsetto register.

In general the modal register has a lower sound and the falsetto a higher sound. It is easy to distinguish between the two registers when we sing; it is not so easy when we speak. When a singer raises the pitch of their voice there is a certain point where they can no longer sing in the modal register without straining. However, if they try to sing the same note quietly, they find they can sing the note, however, there is a different quality to the sound. This is because the tension of the muscles have reached a point where they have to release. This changes the way in which the vocal folds vibrate against each other. Singers who use the falsetto voice learn to control this very precisely. The point at which this occurs is called the 'break point'.

However, the primary function of the vocal folds is not to make sound. The production of sound is a secondary function. Put your finger back on your Adam's apple and swallow. Do you notice how the Adam's apple moves upwards in much the same way as it did when you made the siren sound?

Lying on top of the vocal folds is another pair of folds known as the vestibular folds. Together with the epiglottis (a flap made of elastic cartilage at the base of the tongue) they come together to create a seal. This closes off the trachea to allow food to go down the oesophagus into the stomach, rather than down the trachea into our lungs. This closing movement also occurs when we are in a state of high anxiety. In these emotional states the movement of the Adam's apple is the same as when we are raising the pitch of our voice. Consequently when we are nervous, anxious, angry, stressed out, and trying to speak at the same time, the pitch of our voice becomes higher, it may move into the falsetto register, or it may just stop producing sound altogether. This is why it is sometimes difficult to speak when we are angry, scared or nervous. This was what was happening to Jenny when she got nervous and the overall pitch and timbre of her voice had more to do with anxiety than with her physical size.

Maintaining vocal health

At the beginning of the chapter it was pointed out that the voice is an essential tool for communicating thoughts and ideas with the world around us. Many of us depend on a well functioning voice in order do our work. Nevertheless, very few people are ever given any specific training on how to care and develop the voice effectively.

Occupational voice loss is now affecting record numbers of workers in the UK. One quarter of the workforce report problems with their voice. For some people these problems can mean the end of their careers. Based on research from the US it has been estimated that UK businesses lose £200 million each year from occupational voice disorders.[2]

Any Awareness Through Movement lesson will have a positive impact on the way in which the voice is used as optimum voice production requires the support of the whole muscular skeletal system. It is interesting to note that a baby can scream for hours without any noticeable damage on their vocal health, yet a grown adult is likely to damage the voice as soon as they start shouting. This suggests there is even more we can learn from babies than we might imagine.

Jenny attended local Awareness Through Movement classes at the same time as receiving executive and voice coaching. The voice coaching built on what she was learning in the Awareness Through Movement lessons. She developed a greater sense of self-confidence and became much more assured. This had an impact on the tonal quality of her voice which became more resonant and easy to listen to. She did not have to consciously change the sound or pitch of her voice. Sometimes people are encouraged to do this with the risk that it can make them sound inauthentic. She became highly respected in her role and three years later was 'head hunted' to become chief executive in a different organisation.

The Awareness Through Movement lesson at the end of this chapter focuses specifically on supporting the voice. However, it is worth considering some basic tips that will help to maintain vocal health.[3]

- **Do vocal warm ups before using your voice in the work place.**
  The best way to warm up your voice is to sing. Singing uses the voice in a very precise and sustained way. You don't need to be able to sing well to get the benefit, neither do you have to sing in tune. However, five minutes of humming along to your favourite CD or inventing your own tunes will prepare your voice for the day ahead.
- **Drink plenty of water and avoid drinks containing caffeine which have a diuretic affect.**
  If your throat feels dry this almost certainly means your vocal folds are dry, making it more difficult to speak and communicate effectively. As a result your voice will be more prone to strain and damage. Every time you speak you release moisture with your breath, so if you are speaking for a long time you dehydrate. It is important to rehydrate, preferably by drinking water.
- **Breathe through the nose – see also chapter 4: learning to breathe**
  Many people start to breathe through the mouth when they are talking. This often happens because they are slightly nervous or tense. This can increase the levels of anxiety a person is experiencing. Most people find that breathing through the nose is relaxing.

- **Avoid coughing to clear your throat**
  Too much mucous in the throat makes the voice sound indistinct and causes the individual to try to clear their throat by coughing. Coughing can damage the vocal folds so it is important not to clear your throat unnecessarily.
- **Avoid shouting**
  In some situations people feel that they have to shout in order to make themselves heard. Most people need to raise the pitch of their voice to achieve the necessary muscle tension required to increase the volume of their voice. Generally, they place too much strain on their neck muscles. The whole process makes the voice sound shrill and thin and less likely to make an impact.
- **If you have a sore throat or laryngitis avoid whispering as it actually causes more trauma to the larynx than normal speech.**

Awareness Through Movement Lesson: Learning to talk

As mentioned in the text of this chapter, good functioning of the voice is influenced by a number of wide-ranging factors. All of the lessons in this book so far will have an effect on your speaking voice. You may notice a change in the areas that resonate when you first speak after finishing any of the Awareness Through Movement lessons.

There are some specific ways in which Awareness Through Movement can be helpful in effecting your voice. Begin in sitting, comfortably, either in a chair or on the floor.

To begin with speak as if you are recounting to someone what you just did in the past hours. This is in order to listen to the sound of your own voice. Continue to talk and place one hand on your upper chest, just under your collar bones; feel any sensation in the area under your hand. You will probably feel some movement connected to your breathing in and out and you may also be able to feel a slight vibration in the layers of tissue, muscle and even the bones of the ribs. Listen to the sound of your voice: is it at a low, or high pitch? Do you speak slowly or quickly? How would you describe the quality of your voice?

You will be asked to do this again at the finish of this lesson and to notice if anything is different at that point.

- slowly start to roll back on your sitting bones, feeling how this movement shortens the front of your chest, brings your chin closer to your collar bones, and that you look downwards with your eyes.

- continue to repeat this movement and begin to make an "ah" sound at the start of the movement and notice if and when how the sound changes as you roll backwards and as you return to the starting position.

As the front of your neck shortens, the entire vocal apparatus is pushed slightly backwards, reducing the amount of air that can exit through while making a sound. Those who spend a lot of time in a slightly 'slumped' position are placing a constant pressure on their larynx.

Stop and rest.

Sit comfortably and upright again.

- slowly start to roll forwards on your sitting bones, feeling how this movement makes you longer in the front; your chin moves away from your chest and you look upwards.
- continue to repeat this movement and add making an "ah" sound at the start of the movement, sensing any change in the sound as you roll forwards.

Stop and rest.

With this movement, the back of your neck shortens, pushing the entire vocal apparatus forwards and restricting the space for air to pass through the vocal cords with the out-breath.

- roll once backwards on your sitting bones, then forwards on them, and find a place in between the backward and the forward movement where you can remain comfortably upright. You will probably notice that, at this place, your head is balanced on your spine and that there is not any shortening in the front, or back of your neck.

Staying in this comfortable, upright sitting position: – slowly open your jaw, then close it. Notice how far you can open it without straining and pay attention to whether it opens straight downwards, or moves a bit to the right or to the left while opening and closing. Place your fingertips on your cheekbones, close to your ear and you can feel the movement of the lower jaw, the mandible. You will also be able to

(continued)

(continued)

feel if the part of this bone, closest to your ear, touches your right and left fingertips equally while opening and closing your jaw.

Stop and rest.

Don't be surprised if you detect any slight movements to the right or to the left while your jaw is opening and closing. Many people have slight imbalances in the movement of their jaw. This can be the result of a long-standing habit, which can be explored, or due to dental work, or other facial imbalances.

–   let your jaw open again and leave it open at a comfortable distance from your upper teeth, slide your jaw to the right and return it to the middle. Repeat this a number of times, being sure that you keep your jaw open. If you now place your fingertips in front of your ear again, you can feel this movement to the right reflected in the movement of your mandible.

Close your mouth and rest.

–   open your jaw again, leaving it open at a comfortable distance and this time, slide your jaw to the left and back, remembering to keep your jaw open while doing the sliding movement. Repeat this a number of times and try it also while placing your fingertips in front of your ear, to feel the movement in this part of your jawbone, which is close to the joint where it articulates. Does your jaw move as easily or as far to the left as it did to the right?

Close your mouth and rest.

–   open your jaw again, leave it open and slide it once to the right and once to the left, to compare the two directions. And don't be surprised if they are different.

Close your mouth and rest.

By sensing, feeling and becoming aware of any differences in the movement of your jaw to the right and to the left, you can now become interested in observing these differences. For example, do you tend to chew more with one side of your teeth? There are many factors in differences that show up in the movement of the jaw and as you become curious, they will reveal themselves. And just doing these movements will already assist to bring the jaw into balance.

–   place your right hand on your jaw, so that your thumb and your index finger rest on the front of the base of your jaw; place your left hand on your forehead with your fingertips to the right. Holding your jaw and keeping it from moving, rotate your head to the right with your left hand and return it. Be sure that your jaw is not moving and that the movement is of your head, or skull. Repeat this a number of times.

Stop and rest.

This may feel like a very strange movement and it is. The jaw usually moves while your head stays still and with this instruction, you have reversed the usual relationship. The main jaw muscle, the masseter, with which you chew, is being moved from the opposite direction to which it is accustomed. Where it attaches to the head now moves; normally it moves from the attachment to the jaw. This reversal has the effect of freeing up a pattern which is very deeply embedded in your nervous system.

–   place your left hand now to hold your jaw and your right hand on your forehead. Holding your jaw still, rotate your head to the left and repeat this a number of times.

Stop and rest. Then just open your jaw again as you did earlier and notice if this movement has become easier, without trying to increase its range.

–   with your mouth closed, place the tip of your tongue behind your lower teeth and in the middle; now slowly move your tongue along your lower teeth to the right until you reach the back tooth, then return to the middle. Do this a number of times, as if you are 'examining' the inner surface of each tooth. Feel if your tongue has to make a bit more effort to reach the back tooth.

(continued)

(continued)

Stop and rest.

- take your tongue and this time place it in front of your lower teeth, in between your teeth and the inner side of your chin; move your tongue slowly to the right again along the outside surface of your lower teeth. Be sure to reach all the way back to the outside surface of the last tooth and return to the middle.

Stop and rest.

Now, open your jaw and leave it open; move it to the right and back to the middle. Notice if the range or comfort in this direction is different. Compare this with a few movements of your jaw to the left. Is it convincing that your tongue plays an important role in the movement of your jaw?

- place your tongue again behind your lower teeth and in the middle; move your tongue slowly this time to the left, touching the inside surface of each tooth along the way until you reach the last tooth, then return to the middle. Repeat this a number of times and notice if the movement of your tongue to the left is different than when you moved it to the right.

Stop and rest.

- place your tongue in front of your lower teeth and move it slowly to the left, remaining in touch with the outside surface of your lower teeth and reaching all the way to the back tooth, then return to the middle. Do this a number of times.

Stop and rest.

Open your jaw and leave it open; move it to the left and back to the middle. Has the direction to the left also become easier?

Return to listening to yourself talk, as you did at the start of this lesson. Does your voice sound different? Has the pitch altered? Are you speaking with a different pace? When you place your hand on your upper chest, do you feel more vibration? Would you describe the quality of your voice with different words?

Any parts of this lesson can be used separately and could be very useful before making a presentation, or having an important discussion. It will free up the movements of your jaw and will have an effect on your breathing. And may even affect the impression your words will have on others.

Notes

1 Moshe Feldenkrais (1990). *Awareness through movement. Easy to do exercises to improve your posture, vision, imagination, and personal awareness*. New York: HarperCollins.
2 E Vilkman. Voice problems at work: a challenge for occupational health and safety arrangement. *Folia Phoniatrica et Logopaedica*. 52: 120–125.
3 For more detailed information on voice care see www.britishvoiceassociation. org.uk

Conclusion
Moving in all directions

*Any change, improvement, correction made to a habit can feel, both
kinaesthetically and emotionally, like an error in the opposite direction.*[1]
Moshe Feldenkrais

Case story

Jenny is lying on a Feldenkrais table. She has just been asked to
lie on her back with her legs long and her arms by her side. Her
Feldenkrais teacher asks her if she feels that she is lying straight.
She replies that she is. The Feldenkrais practitioner makes a few
adjustments and feeds back to Jenny that she is now lying straight.
Before making the adjustment her right side was extended and she
was about as straight as a croissant.

'Are you seriously telling me that this is straight? It doesn't feel
straight – in fact it feels really odd and slightly uncomfortable.'

Introduction

This book is about a particular way of getting to know one's self – i.e.
through experiencing sensation whilst trying out a variety of slow, easy
and pleasant movements. Some of these movements may be new to you,
others you will have experienced before, many probably in your early
years as a young child. Developing awareness through movement is
incredibly empowering and will have a beneficial effect not only upon
your own performance and wellbeing but also anyone else you introduce
the Method to. The principles of the Feldenkrais Method can be applied
in practise whilst undertaking any other activity. Once a person starts to

develop awareness through movement it can be consciously applied in everything that person does.

At the beginning of this book it was emphasised that the Feldenkrais Method was not being promoted as an 'instead of' approach to personal development. That would be an error as there are a multitude of practical tools and models that have been designed and have proved to be efficacious in their application. What the Feldenkrais Method does offer is an experiential way that develops the awareness that is often required to apply the theoretical models that many coaches, learning and development specialists, and managers use in their work.

However, in order to get the most from this book it is worth considering four themes that recur frequently throughout – namely: action; curiosity; habit; and, awareness.

Action

'Every action we undertake consists of the following elements – thinking, feeling (emotion), sensation, and movement.'

This statement has appeared in most chapters throughout this book. Quite simply this is because behind this statement lies the underlying principle that makes the Feldenkrais Method work. Whilst Moshe Feldenkrais was adamant that no element could be addressed in isolation of another, the easiest way to promote personal growth was through the study of one's movement. This was based on his observation that the majority of the central nervous system was predominantly engaged with movement.

Whilst reading this book is by definition an action, the movement aspect of reading is not necessarily the pre-dominant element. In order to fully experience the book a person needs to undertake and experience the lessons that have been offered. This requires a degree of curiosity.

Curiosity

'Does it really work?' asked an early reviewer of this book.

'Have you tried the Awareness Through Movement lessons at the end of each chapter?' was the reply.

'Oh no, I haven't had time to do that, that's why I am asking.'

Hopefully, if you have arrived at this final chapter you will have read the previous chapters leading up to it. If you have, then the question is this – have you been curious enough to attempt the lessons?

More often than not there is a tendency to read a book such as this and happily ignore the practical experiential activities it contains. However, unless we try out these activities there is no way that we can verify what has been illustrated. The difference between knowledge and understanding is in the application of what has been read. A person may read about bee keeping and have the knowledge, however, they will only have understanding when they actually keep bees.

What is the motivating influence that would encourage a person to try out the lessons in this book? For the people being coached it could well be the prospect of achieving a promotion, or being able to present to over a thousand sales executives at a conference. Then what? Does personal development stop at that point of achievement?

Moshe Feldenkrais constantly reiterated the need for curiosity. Without curiosity we can take our behaviours for granted. Without curiosity we don't question the perceived wisdom of the day. Without curiosity there is no discovery. Without curiosity we will not learn anything new. Personal development is life long – hence life long learning. Maybe what we need to develop is the habit of curiosity.

The nature of habit

In one way or another habits have been mentioned frequently in this book. However, it is important not to give the acquisition of habits a bad press. There are useful habits and there are habits that may be less beneficial than others and then there are the new habits we may acquire that enable us to become more efficient in what we do.

A habit is a familiar way of thinking, feeling, and moving that is developed through repetition. However, it is within the nature of a habit that it can function without any self-awareness of what is being undertaken. This in itself may not be a bad thing as it allows a person to multi-task. However, the lack of awareness may also result in a lack of curiosity. It is still important to be able to question if the habit is the most efficient way of doing an activity. Has the habit limited our choice of action in any way? Is that habit beneficial to our life?

Developing new habits

As anyone who has made a new year's resolution to go to fitness classes will tell you, developing a new habit is not easy. According to research it can take on average 66 days to acquire one.[2] Equally it can be assumed that it takes the equivalent amount of time to relinquish an old habit that is no longer beneficial to us. However many of our habits feel comfortable, including those habitual emotions, postures and movements developed over many years in our life. Any correction may feel incorrect to begin with. Jenny's initial discomfort at the shift her Feldenkrais teacher suggested was due to an unconscious habit of holding herself in a certain manner, which, over the years, had become natural to her – it had become her image of herself. Some people with severe postural difficulties that have resulted in years of pain, do not want to be changed. Their pain has become part of who they are and how they see themselves in relationship to their environment. They are quite reasonably afraid of a life without pain which would require them to redefine their relationship with the world. Perversely they are comfortable with their discomfort. Likewise, and to a lesser extent, many of us become comfortable as we are. We have our habitual ways of working, our favourite psychological models of engagement, and our beliefs that what we are doing is the right and only way of doing it.

Curiosity engages our awareness. It enables us to become interested in what we are doing and why we are doing it. It enables our individual personal development and increases our choice of behaviours.

In answer to the question – does it work? Yes, for many of us who have tasted the method Moshe Feldenkrais developed, Awareness Through Movement works. It enables us to explore our habits on both a kinaesthetic and emotional basis. It stimulates our curiosity. It develops our self awareness. It will help us develop our performance in any way we wish. It enables us to respond to what is going on around us rather than react. It also enhances our health and wellbeing as individuals.

Awareness Through Movement

In Chapter 3, Moshe Feldenkrais describing ideal posture was quoted saying: 'you want to be able to move in all of the cardinal directions – forwards, backwards; upwards, downwards; to the right and to the left – without needing to make a preliminary reorganisation.' This is efficiency in movement – being able to 'move in all directions' as necessary and as the need arises. In order to achieve this a certain degree of alertness is required, or in other words, a state of self-awareness of our surroundings at all times.

Some people question the need for this degree of alertness, arguing that constantly 'thinking' about what is going on around them places restriction on effective performance and 'slows them down'. Alertness is not 'thinking' – it is the conscious sensation of self that is aware and alive to the present moment. It is in the present moment that all action occurs, including planning for the future.

It is the lack of self-awareness that results in ill health, stress, and those unfortunate impulsive reactions such as John and Bill experienced in Chapter 1.

Some people will argue that they do not have enough time during the day to concern themselves with developing their self-awareness. The reality is that self-awareness is generated through the habit of curiosity and whilst it requires an element of time to develop the habit, once the habit has been developed it can be applied in all our activities without too much effort. A colleague once commented that all learning and development could be distilled as the need for self-awareness. It can't. Curiosity is also fed by the acquisition of knowledge and new skills. The workplace needs all the theories relating to leadership and the management of others. People need to be able to invent and develop solutions to everyday problems.

As stated at the beginning of this book the Feldenkrais Method offers an additional approach to coaching that can be used for personal development. It is our hope that this book will encourage you to explore what the Feldenkrais Method has to offer.

Notes

1 Taken from the Amherst Training 17th June 1981.
2 Lally, P, van Jaarsveld, C H M, Potts, H W W and Wardle, J (2010). How are habits formed: modelling habit formation in the real world. European Journal of Social Psychology, 40: 998–1009. doi:10.1002/ejsp.674.

Resources

Books by Moshe Feldenkrais

Body and mature behavior: a study of anxiety, sex, gravitation, and learning. (2005). Originally published in 1949 by Routledge & Kegan Paul. Berkeley, CA: Frog Books and Somatic Resources. ISBN 1-583941-15-0.

Awareness through movement: easy to do exercises to improve your posture, vision, imagination, and personal awareness. (1990). New York: HarperCollins. ISBN 978-0-06-250322-0.

Body awareness as healing therapy: the case of Nora. (1993). Berkeley, CA: Frog Books and Somatic Resources. ISBN 1-883319-08-0.

The elusive obvious. (1981). Capitola, CA: Meta Publications. ISBN 978-0-91-699009-1.

The master moves. (1989). Capitola, CA: Meta Publications. ISBN 0-916990-15-X.

The potent self: a study of compulsion and spontaneity. (2002). Berkeley, CA: Frog Books and Somatic Resources. ISBN 1-58394-068-5

Embodied wisdom: The collected papers of Moshe Feldenkrais, edited by Elizabeth Beringer. (2010). Berkeley, CA: North Atlantic Books. ISBN 978-1-55643-906-3.

Organisations

The Feldenkrais Guild UK. The professional organisation of practitioners and teachers in the UK.

www.feldenkrais.co.uk The International Feldenkrais Federation.

www.feldenkrais-method.org The Feldenkrais International Training Centre.

Based in the UK the centre provides practitioner training and other courses for the general public.

www.feldenkrais-itc.com

Index

Printed in the United States
by Baker & Taylor Publisher Services